PRAYING
THE BIBLE

for

YOUR LIFE

DAVID KOPP

WATERBROOK
PRESS

PRAYING THE BIBLE FOR YOUR LIFE
PUBLISHED BY WATERBROOK PRESS
5446 North Academy Boulevard, Suite 200
Colorado Springs, Colorado 80918
A division of Random House, Inc.

Portions of this work were originally published in *Praying the Bible for Your Children*
and *Praying the Bible for Your Marriage* by David and Heather Kopp, copyright 1997,
published by WaterBrook Press.

ISBN 1-57856-136-1

Library of Congress Cataloging-in-Publication Data
Kopp, David, 1949–
    Praying the Bible for your life / David Kopp. — 1st ed.
        p.   cm.
    Includes bibliographical references and index.
    ISBN 1-57856-136-1 (hb)
    1. Prayers. 2. Bible—Devotional use. I. Title.
BS245.K66 1999
242'.5—dc21   99-21781
                                                                              CIP

Printed in the United States of America
1999—First Edition

10 9 8 7 6 5 4 3 2 1

In Memory of
Charles Joseph Kopp,
Dad

I thank my God every time I remember you.

PHILIPPIANS 1:3

Contents

An Invitation

The prayer book you are holding is composed almost entirely of Scripture-based prayers, personalized for your devotional use. It is especially for you if you've ever thought, *My prayer life feels stuck. If I bore myself, how must God be feeling?* Or, *My prayers seem weak and ineffective. How can I pray with more confidence and power?*

Intentionally praying the Bible can bring a whole new dimension to our relationship with God. As a pastor from an earlier time wrote, "Through the Bible God talks to us, and through prayer we talk to God. Few of us are ever prepared to speak to God, until God has spoken to us by His Word."[1] Think of these prayers then as living, two-way conversations. By reflecting attentively on Scripture as we pray, we let the words and desires of Christ come to rich life within us (Col. 3:16). And we understand in a new way the simple petition of François Fénelon: "Lord, I know not what I ought to ask of thee; thou only knowest what I need. Teach me to pray. Pray thyself in me."[2]

As with the previous books in the Praying the Bible series, my hope is that these written prayers will help you express your own deepest desires and encourage you forward in the most important conversation of your life.

DAVID KOPP

CHAPTER 1

The Conversation of Your Life

My heart trembles at your word. I rejoice in your promise like one who finds great spoil.

PSALM 119:161-162

Prayer—conversation with God—is so simple that it can be understood and experienced by a five-year-old. And the urge to pray—at least to whisper "Keep him safe" or "Help me, God"—is so basic to living that most of us can hardly tell where breathing ends and praying begins. (Since Heather and I have five teenagers between us, we take our breathing pretty seriously!)

So why is it that so often when we set out to pray consistently and effectively for ourselves and those we love most, we find ourselves becoming tongue-tied, repetitious, dull? Why is what we remember about our praying the sound of our own worried askings, not a sense of the Father's presence and pleasure, much less the sound of His voice in return?

Deep down, we want more. We want to pray in a way that makes a difference in us, those we love, and our world. We want to deeply enjoy God's presence, receive His blessings, and become a little more like Jesus every day. We want a prayer life that works.

Fortunately for us humans, God is deeply committed to His end of the conversation. In fact, as A. W. Tozer has pointed out, our impulse to pursue God originates with God. "We pursue God because, and only because, He has first put an urge within us that spurs us to the pursuit. 'No man can come to me,' said our Lord, 'except the Father which hath sent me draw him.'"[1]

The good news is that our Father always wants to talk. If we're willing listeners and learners, He coaches us all our lives long. It shouldn't surprise us then that when we turn to the Bible itself for help, we find the "more" we've been looking for.

GOD'S PRAYER BOOK

The Bible is a ready-made prayer book for God's family. We "pray the Bible" when we use passages of Scripture to form prayers, or when we say the verses directly back to God, making them our own petitions. Jesus said, "If you remain in me and my words remain in you, ask whatever you wish, and it will be given you" (John 15:7). Whenever we speak to God with the words of God, we move closer to the kind of vital, effective prayer life we long for.

Several years ago I realized that I'd been praying the Bible all my life—I'd just never called it that. My dad, Joe Kopp, had grown up with a passion for reciting Bible verses, partly as a way to overcome a serious speech impediment. But it was a passion that would shape his life and ministry. Bed-bound for a week during seminary, he memorized the book of Hebrews. When he and my mother went to central Africa as missionaries in 1945, Dad relied on Bible memorization to teach pre-literate Africans the Bible and help them grow in their new faith. People called Joe Kopp "the Man of the Book." Saying Bible passages back to God became part of every village church service, and part of our home life, too.

We grew up learning Scripture around the breakfast table. Even though Dad's been with the Lord for twenty years now, the legacy he left us persists. My brother Tom wrote recently: "I still have memories of us sitting around the table. Dad would say, 'Again!' and we'd repeat the verse yet again. Then it would be, 'Now, Tom, you say it.' And then, 'Okay, all together now.' And now when I read those verses, I can close my eyes and hear Dad's voice."

That's the heart of praying Scripture. In it we hear most clearly our Father's voice.

In a very natural way, Dad would turn the promises from the day's verse into thanksgiving or petitions as he prayed with us around that table or at bedtime. And Mom claimed—and still does—a life verse for each of her offspring. I've never forgotten Mom's prayer for me, or the twinkle of confidence in her eye when she reminds me of it. "Honey, I'm confident of this, that He who began a good work in you will carry it on to completion!" (from Phil. 1:6).

With a heritage like this, Heather and I have done our best to make the Bible and Scripture prayers a part of our life together. The opportunities for praying the Bible are so varied:

- a promise when considering a job or career decision: "Lord, You will fulfill Your purpose for me. Your love for me endures for-ever—and You never abandon the works of Your hands" (from Ps. 138:8).

- a prayer of encouragement for a spouse: "Today I claim these promises from You for my wife: 'My kindness, mercies, and love for Heather are inexhaustible!'" (from Isa. 54:8; Deut. 13:17; Jer. 31:3).

- a screen-saver prayer for our boys: "Lord, help us to be on guard today, to stand firm in the faith, to be men of courage, to be strong, and to do everything in love" (from 1 Cor. 16:13-14).

- a praise from Scripture written in chalk on the inside of the foundation of our house: "The LORD is good, a refuge in times of trouble. He cares for those who trust in him" (Nah. 1:7).

That's just one family's example. But praying the Bible is as old as the Bible itself. Jesus often used Scripture in His prayers for Himself and His disciples. Throughout the Bible, we see examples of godly men and women incorporating God's promises and commands in their petitions to Him. They used the Word in their prayers for encouragement, calling to mind who God is and what He has done. Jesus and His disciples sang the psalms together as part of morning and evening prayers. And at the moment of His greatest agony on the cross, Jesus cried out the words of a psalm: "My God, my God, why have you forsaken me?" (Ps. 22:1).

Many other Bible passages are recorded prayers. Some of the best known are the prayer of Moses after the escape through the Red Sea (Exodus 15); Hannah's song at the temple (1 Samuel 2); Jeremiah's lament over Jerusalem (Lamentations); Jonah's plea for grace (Jonah 2); the song of Mary after the angel's visit (Luke 1:46-55); the Lord's Prayer (Matt. 6:9-13); Jesus' prayer for his disciples (John 17:6-19); and Paul's prayers for a young church (Eph. 3:14-21).

Since the time of Christ, Christians throughout the world have used the book of Psalms as an unofficial prayer book for the church. Prayer books designated for public worship contain some of our most enduring examples of Scripture-based prayers. For example, one form of the Great Thanksgiving, from *The Book of Common Prayer*, is taken from Romans 12:1-2: "And here we offer and present unto thee, O Lord, our selves, our souls and bodies, to be a reasonable, holy, and living sacrifice unto thee."[2] The Jesus Movement of the 1970s brought back singing choruses of Scripture as a vibrant part of church worship in many circles.

Praying the Bible for Your Life applies this principle to personal prayer. C. S. Lewis, among many others, used written, Bible-based prayers in his devotional life. Lewis said this helped him concentrate, stay doctrinally sound, and know how to pray. Otherwise, he said, "the crisis of the present moment, like the nearest telegraph post, will always loom largest."[3]

HOW TO PRAY EFFECTIVELY

Every day we face crises small and large. In the face of them, we often lack faith, asking God repeatedly for what he has already promised. Or we ramble and whine—and sometimes give up altogether. At these times, the Bible can help us find more meaningful and effective expressions for this holy conversation, and rescue us from some of our limitations.

But where should we start? With the simple principles for talking with God that the Bible lays down. The Holy Spirit can help us make them part of a successful prayer experience.

Pray reverently. Keep in mind God's holiness and greatness. Pray with genuine respect and humility (Eccles. 5:1-2; Matt. 6:9).

Pray sincerely. The words don't matter as much as your heart. Bring a deeply felt desire to see God act, and a wholehearted willingness to do your part to make God's solutions possible (Matt. 6:7-8; Heb. 10:22; Ps. 51:17).

Pray in faith. Simply and completely trust in God's desire for your best interests and in His power to act on your behalf (Jer. 32:17; Heb. 11:6).

Pray with purity. Don't let your prayers be hindered by known sin in your heart or life: unfinished business with God, your neighbor, or your own family members (Prov. 15:8; Mark 12:38-40; 1 John 3:21-22; 1 Peter 3:7).

Pray according to God's will. Submit your personal desires to God's greater glory and purposes. Test your wishes against His revealed truth (1 John 5:14; Matt. 6:10).

Pray in Jesus' name. We have access to the Father through Jesus' name and by His merits. His name is the power above all powers on earth (John 15:16; Eph 2:18).

Pray thankfully. Recalling God's past goodness and His faithful character, surround every new request with thanksgiving and praise (Phil. 4:6; Ps. 22:3).

Pray boldly and persistently. Jesus taught that a loving Father is waiting to give us His best, and it's better than we could ever imagine. Make your requests known, and continue to expect answers (Heb. 4:16; Luke 18:1-8; Acts 12:5).

These are the kinds of conversations God promises to favor with His presence and His answers. Good praying is, after all, the sound God's family makes. The spectrum of that sound includes praise, thanksgiving, confession, petition, intercession, worship—the wonderful hubbub of earnest talking and listening between children and their heavenly Father.

If we're willing to practice the few rules of prayer, we can benefit from the many freedoms:

- We can pray anywhere, anytime (Jon. 2:1; 2 Tim. 1:3).

- We can wail out our deepest, most unpleasant feelings and know God will not be shocked or deaf to our pleas (Ps. 102:17; Lam. 2:19).
- We can pray haltingly, simply, confusedly (Rom. 8:26; Ps. 69:33).
- We can pray alone or with other believers (Dan. 6:10; Acts 2:42-47).
- We can pray ecstatically, carried along by the Spirit, or woodenly, driven by our commitments when all feelings fail us (Eph. 5:18-19; Ps. 102:23-28).
- We can pray silently, wordlessly (Ps. 5:1; Matt. 6:6).
- We can pray over and over for the same thing, confident we'll never be tuned out (Luke 18:1-8).

Praying the Bible for Your Life celebrates yet another rewarding freedom in our praying: We can speak the words and wishes of God back to Him, making them the sincerest expression of our own hearts (Col. 3:16).

WAYS TO PRAY SCRIPTURE

The ways to pray Scripture start with letting psalms and Bible prayers speak for us. But that's just a beginning. For example, we can:
- personalize a Bible prayer: "O Father, no matter how hard I try (and sometimes I don't try at all), I can't stay ahead of my debts—the ways I've injured and disappointed others, my convenient omissions and forgetfulness, my constant turning away from You. Forgiveness is my only hope. Teach me today..."

(Praying the Lord's Prayer, "Forgive us our debts, as we also have forgiven our debtors," Matt. 6:12-15.)

- personalize a Bible promise: "Lord, You live in a high and holy place, but also with the person who is contrite and lowly in spirit (from Isa. 57:15). Thank You. Show me anything in my heart or life that grieves You. Your gracious presence is all I need."

- personalize a Bible story: "Dear Lord Jesus, because You argued with lawyers and experts, with seekers and doubters; because You stayed up late into the night to answer dumb questions from one seeking soul who couldn't quite grasp what 'born again' could possibly mean, but wanted to—I pray today for the ones I know who need so desperately to be saved." (Praying from the story of Nicodemus, John 3.)

- personalize a Bible statement as a response from God: "Lord, I hardly believe in prayer today. I'm sorry." *What is impossible with men is possible with God* (Luke 18:27). "Yes, prayer seems so impossible, Lord. How can I, all human, converse with God—all Spirit, all power, all knowledge, all good?" *Draw near to God and He will draw near to you* (James 4:8, NASB).

- personalize a Bible truth as a meditation: "I am always welcome in my Father's presence today—no matter what!" (from Heb. 10:19-22).

As we acknowledge and agree with God's truth, our praying takes on new life. Real conversation replaces venting. Our fixations with what we want drop away as in their place a relationship unfolds. God Himself comes in. As Mother Teresa once wrote: "Prayer enlarges the heart until it is capable of containing God's gift of himself. Ask and seek, and your heart will grow big enough to receive him and to keep him as your own."[4]

When we pray with the Bible as our guide, we're intentionally setting about to enlarge our heart for God. Consider some ways praying Scripture can work for us:

Praying the Bible gets us "unstuck." Sometimes we're not diligent in prayer because we have a record of mediocre experiences with it—we get distracted, bored, vague. Mostly we have a hard time getting started. Words and ideas fail us. Praying intentionally with Scripture in mind is like choosing to follow a map in new territory. Suddenly you can spot several worthy destinations. You can pray confidently and specifically: "Thank You that as I make You Lord of my future, You'll show me step by step how to make the right decisions" (from Prov. 3:6).

Praying the Bible helps us get our memory back. Sometimes we feel so overwhelmed by feelings and needs that our prayers don't seem to reach beyond the problem. We forget God's character, His promises, His past faithfulness and goodness, even His extravagances with us. Praying the truths of the Bible helps us remember what God has done and what He can still do.

Jeremiah was an emotional priest called to speak for God during the siege and fall of Jerusalem. When he focused on the terrors around him, Jeremiah felt personally assaulted, even abandoned by God: "He pierced my heart with arrows from his quiver" (Lam. 3:13). Only when he focused on God's past mercies did he find strength and encouragement: "Yet this I call to mind and therefore I have hope: Because of the LORD's great love we are not consumed, for his compassions never fail" (3:21-22).

Praying the Bible helps us pray more specifically and in line with

God's will. Without intending to, we can pray ignorantly, even at cross-purposes with what God wants. Jesus told the Pharisees, "You are in error because you do not know the Scriptures or the power of God" (Matt. 22:29). In the same way we use the Bible to measure the content of a sermon or lesson, we can use Scripture to test our motives and reveal the big picture. When we pray the Bible back to God, we speak to God in the words of God with the truth of God. This encourages us to go beyond "Lord, help me to get along with the people at work" to a more complete expression: "Lord, You ask me to show respect to persons in authority and to make peacemaking and faithfulness, not getting ahead, my priorities (1 Tim. 2:1-2; James 3:17-18; 1 Cor. 4:2). But my pride keeps me on the defensive, protecting my position or reputation or rights. My pride—a false and exaggerated sense of my own importance—is offensive to You (Prov. 8:13). I'm truly sorry. Please forgive me and show me a better way today."

In this kind of prayer, we bring God's revealed will into our thoughts, not just our problem or our wishes for a resolution. And when we pray in line with God's will, He promises to answer (1 John 5:14).

Praying the Bible helps us pray with confidence and expectancy. When we know and use biblical truth, we can pray with a more muscular faith. Faith is not a belief that "anything can happen," writes Wayne Spear, but a confidence that what God has promised will happen.[5] When we pray in harmony with the principles of Scripture, we can be sure that our needs will be met even though we leave the how and when to God.

Praying the Bible helps us nurture a growing relationship with God. Prayer is an ongoing conversation between two very interested parties, and the Bible is God's recorded end of the conversation. Imagine a young couple who becomes engaged only to be suddenly separated for months by the man's military service. Every day the man sends his fiancée a lengthy letter telling her about his daily activities, describing his hopes and dreams for their future, and declaring the depth of his affection for her. But when the couple finally reunites, they soon find themselves lapsing unaccountably into silences. Finally the young woman complains that she hardly knows her suitor. "I'm not even sure how much you really care about me!" she exclaims. After some painful probing, the truth comes out: The woman has never actually read her mail. "Usually I just opened the letters to see if you still signed off 'with love,'" she admits. "And, well, then I put them in a safe place…"

When we neglect to bring Scripture into our prayer conversation, we can be as confused about who God is as this woman was about her husband-to-be. We struggle needlessly with doubts about God's intentions toward us, simply because we haven't read, believed, or remembered His love letter to us.

Praying the Bible can open our hearts to allow the Spirit to minister to us. Scripture leads us into an encounter with the Father-heart of God. We hear our Father's voice: "Fear not, for I have redeemed you; I have summoned you by name; you are mine" (Isaiah 43:1). And we bask in His presence. This is the attitude David describes in Psalm 131:2: "I have stilled and quieted my soul; like a weaned child with its mother." Scriptures like this remind us that we're invited to come to God with nothing to give, only with who we are—listening, surrendering, perhaps broken and in need of comfort or healing. Henri Nouwen described this kind of receptivity as "praying with open hands," an act of devotion that he said often requires greater courage but promises a more enduring result.[6]

Praying the Bible doesn't mean we have to leave out our untidy humanness when we talk with God. The Bible leads us toward the truth about our humanity, not away from it. Consider how many of David's psalms begin with a cry from the depths of his very human soul. Paul repeatedly asked God to free him from his "thorn in his flesh." Even Jesus begged God to "take this cup from me." God longs for honest communication with us. Unlike the cashier at the grocery store, when God asks, "How are you today?" He really wants to know. Of course, we can't hide our real thoughts and feelings from God anyway. Yet because we come to God through Christ's righteousness, we approach confidently, sure that God receives us with grace regardless of our faults (Heb. 10:19-22).

Praying the Bible is not about using fancy language or sounding "religious." In Matthew 6, Jesus warned about praying aloud just to look more "spiritual" to others, and about bombarding God with excess words in hopes that He will hear us better. We don't need to "talk better" to be acceptable to God, nor can we manipulate or impress Him with our carefully worded prayers. The true test of our praying lies in our simple faith and a pure devotion to God's will.

Praying the Bible doesn't mean we always get what we want. Scholars cite 650 prayers in the Bible (outside the book of Psalms, which forms a prayer book of its own), and 450 of these prayers have recorded answers. What, we wonder, makes some prayers "work" while others don't appear to?

At times we must go forward in faith when God's answers to deeply felt concerns remain wrapped in mystery. We pray "magically" when we believe that a certain arrangement of words, like the right coins inserted in a vending machine, will guarantee the same result every time. It's true that we have access to power in Jesus' name, that we receive power through God's Word, and that we can release God's power through our faith. But we don't ever leverage God or control His will, no matter how we pray. Our fallen world comes complete with chaos, tragedy, uncertainty, randomness, and personal trials of all kinds. Jesus' promise to us is not that we can magically escape them through prayer, but that we can overcome them (John 16:33).

MAKING THESE PRAYERS YOUR OWN

In the prayers that follow, you'll find Scripture-based prayers in a variety of formats. References in the text point the way to the Bible passage at hand. The words of the Bible are used as is or modified slightly for personal application, or the prayer addresses a given passage or collection of verses. Some of the meditations are brief enough to memorize easily or to copy onto paper and slip into a briefcase, backpack, or handbag.

In an effort to represent a range of concerns, I identified ten subject categories to write about: character traits, protection and deliverance, wisdom and guidance, emotional and relationship needs, blessing and provision, thanks and praise, confession, intercession for others, spiritual growth and Christian living, and intimacy with God. You can use the indexes to help you track down a prayer either by title or by topic.

A handful of prayers on marriage and children have been picked up from Heather's and my previous books on these subjects, and some other previously published prayers have served as starting points for new ones here.

I encourage you to keep *Praying the Bible for Your Life* on your nightstand or on your desk and to use it as part of your daily devotional time. As you invest yourself in prayer in new ways, may the Holy Spirit use this book to encourage you and move you quickly "beyond reading into praying."[7]

Here's my prayer for you:

Heavenly Father,

In Jesus' name, I pray—and am confident—that You will give endurance, encouragement, and hope to the reader who is about to use these pages in conversation with You (Rom. 15:5,13). May every printed and uttered word that is true spring up to new life; may every word that is false blow away and be forgotten.

I thank You, Lord, that You will accomplish immeasurably more than all I could ask or imagine for this praying reader (Eph. 3:20). Thank You so much that You want to be known by Your children and that You lend us Your own resurrection power to help make it happen (Ps. 25:14; 1 Peter 1:21).

Yes, teach this earnest disciple to pray, and answer every prayer for his or her extravagant good, as only You can (Luke 11:1; 1 John 5:14-15; Rom. 8:28). May Your living words, Your indescribable peace, and Your awesome presence flourish in his or her life for all to see (Col. 3:15-16).

How good it is to seek You and to wait for Your reply (Lam. 3:25-26)! I love You and praise You, Father! I pray these things for Your honor, for Your will in the world, and for the blessings that You want to share with the reader now.

Amen.

DAILY PRAYERS

"Ask," You Said

Ask and it will be given to you; seek and you will find; knock and the door will be opened to you.

LUKE 11:9

Lord Jesus, radical teacher, soul friend, and God—
"Ask," You said.

Jesus, I ask for physical strength and healing today. I ask for success in my work and my relationships. I ask for peace in my heart. I ask for protection and blessing for the ones I love.

Jesus, what do You want me to ask for today?

(I wait and listen.)

"Seek," You said.

Jesus, I seek smart and good choices today. I seek a life of significance and fulfillment. I seek to become all that You've made me to be. I seek a fuller awareness of Your presence with me each moment.

Jesus, what do You want me to seek today?

(I wait and listen.)

"Knock," You said.

Jesus, I knock on the unknowns of my life for understanding. I knock on opportunities for personal growth and career advancement. I knock on new relationships for friendship and comfort. I knock and knock…because You put eternity in my heart, but the clock is always ticking.

Jesus, what doors do You want me to knock on today?

(I wait and listen.)

Today, Lord Jesus—friend of plain folks with grubby little wants and needs—I want to obey Your teaching. Now please do as You have promised—give, reveal, open. Do these things as You think best. I'll wait and watch and give thanks. I don't want just lollipops when You have life to give away.

Thank You, Jesus—teacher, friend, and Lord.

Amen.

Holy Desires

Sometimes God gives us the desires of our hearts to teach us that it is possible to famish while we feed, that these desires gratify self but send leanness to the soul. In fact, if we ask God for anything, only desiring to get pleasure out of it, we are asking on a low level. For prayer is God answering His own desires: that is, desires begotten in the soul by God the Holy Spirit which are presented in the name of God the Son and answered by God the Father.

A. W. TOZER

Map, Suitcase, Phone Number

At the LORD's command they encamped, and at the LORD's command they set out.

NUMBERS 9:23

Heavenly Father,

I bring to You today my "need" to know the future, to have everything in hand to guarantee success. You've blessed me with skills, work experience, and motivation. And most days I want to use these tools to collect assets—a nice house, the right friends, a fat bank account, a stellar career.

But today I hear You asking me to give these gifts back to You. To put them down in faith, and instead to pick up map, suitcase, and phone number.

Like Your people crossing the Sinai desert, help me to listen for Your directions, whether it's "Camp here" or "Move on." Thank You, Father, that Your voice in my ear is the only map I need (Isa. 30:21).

During those times when I feel like a turtle trying to learn to fly—have patience, Father. Teach me the liberating principles of resting in You and of packing light (Isa. 30:15). May my suitcase contain only the essentials of love and obedience (1 Sam. 15:22; Mark 12:33). I want to be like Abraham, who, "when called to go to a place he would later receive as his inheritance, obeyed and went, even though he did not know where he was going" (Heb. 11:8).

And when I'm exhausted and feel lost in my life, let the first call I make be in prayer to You. I know that You will always answer me when I call. For You have promised, "My Presence will go with you, and I will give you rest" (Exod. 33:14). Thank You, Lord!

Amen.

Power Burst

Even youths grow tired and weary, and young men stumble and fall; but those who hope in the LORD will renew their strength. They will soar on wings like eagles; they will run and not grow weary, they will walk and not be faint.

ISAIAH 40:30-31

Lord,

I pray today for those times when I've pushed too hard and nothing's left. That's when I'm prone to discouragement and unhelpful thoughts, attitudes, and behaviors. I gasp with the psalmist, "My heart pounds, my strength fails me; even the light has gone from my eyes" (Ps. 38:10). But You are my source of strength (Ps. 27:1).

Lord, when my strength is gone, be strength for me. When I get to the end of my rope, meet me there with Your grace—completely sufficient, free, saving—amazing (John 1:16; Eph. 1:6-7)!

When I hit the wall because of disobedience to You, show me the riches of mercy and freedom to be found in You through confession and restoration (Prov. 28:13).

When I fall because I have pridefully trusted in my own wisdom or strength, help me reach out in trust to You again (Prov. 3:5-6).

And when You discipline me for a season, may I receive it as a painful-but-priceless gift from the hand of a loving Father (Heb. 12:10).

Thank You for the assurance that whatever my day brings, or whatever You put before me, You'll give me the strength I need (Deut. 33:25; Phil. 4:13).

Come to Me, all who are weary and heavy-laden, and I will give you rest (Matt. 11:28, NASB).

Amen.

Smooth Operators

In fact, everyone who wants to live a godly life in Christ Jesus will be
persecuted, while evil men and impostors will go from bad to worse,
deceiving and being deceived.

2 TIMOTHY 3:12-13

Heavenly Father,

Lately it seems that impostors have gone from bad to worse, just like
Paul warned. What some people do in Your name doesn't seem to agree
at all with what Your Word says You want. Give them a publisher, Web
site, or TV program, and they're able to assail and deceive millions.

Father, You see the powerbrokers who don't fear You. You see the
smooth operators with their bestsellers and Christian trinkets and Ital-
ian suits and fake Louis XIV furniture. They spout Your name while
fleecing gullible believers. They pander to the guilt, fear, and good
intentions of others instead of humbly sharing the gospel.

Will You bring justice, Lord? Will You rise up today to defend Your
own name from Your own people? Please do. Forgive me if I slander any
of those who genuinely serve You. But I want to be zealous for Your reputation—starting in my own life (2 Tim. 2:15). I'm not ashamed of Your
gospel (Rom. 1:16)! But, honestly, some of Your people give me the creeps.

Help me to look to You today, to listen to Your quiet, firm directions in my life, and to "live a godly life in Christ Jesus." Show me
where I can be an example and a force for integrity. And, Father, help
me leave the other family business to You.

Maintain justice and do what is right, for my salvation is close at hand
and my righteousness will soon be revealed (Isa. 56:1).

Amen.

Green Pastures, Still Waters

He maketh me to lie down in green pastures: he leadeth me beside the still waters.

PSALM 23:2, KJV

PRAYING PSALM 23

Shepherd of my life,

I bless You and praise You. You stand watch over my life—all its petty concerns and perpetual wanderings—with Your calm, strong care. All around I see green pastures today; all inside, still waters. Thank You.

Great Shepherd, because You take my needs as Your personal concern, I'll never be without what I truly need (v. 1). I love You.

You lead me every day into places and experiences where my soul will be restored, where my strength to follow You will be renewed (vv. 2-3). Thank You, gentle provider.

When daily burdens press me down, or fears of danger or death cast a shadow over my way, You stay with me. You carry me along, comfort me, keep nudging me toward maturity (v. 4). Your presence and power are my constant companions. How I praise You!

Possessive Lord, I've even noticed this: When I'm cornered by Your enemies, You lavish abundance on me right under their noses. You want the world to know I'm Your chosen one, the pick of the flock (v. 5).

Dear Shepherd, I thank You that Your unfailing goodness and extravagant mercies will surround me the rest of my life—until the moment I'm rolling in the green grass of heaven, my eternal home (v. 6).

Lord of green pastures, Spirit of still waters, I exalt only You!
Amen.

Spiritual Delinquent

I am like a deaf man, who cannot hear, like a mute, who cannot open his mouth;... I wait for You, O LORD; you will answer, O Lord my God.

PSALM 38:13,15

Lord,

I hardly believe in prayer today. I'm sorry.

I'm human—made of bones and cravings, of wandering thoughts and a weak spirit. How can I converse with God—all Spirit, all power, all knowledge, all good?

Come near to God and he will come near to you (James 4:8).

But You seem so far away. I can't feel You or hear Your voice. And when I come near, I'm assaulted with distractions, with accusations, with the uncomfortable awareness that You shouldn't trust a word I say.

Be still, and know that I am God (Ps. 46:10).

Have mercy, Lord, but maybe it's not You I want today. "Wanting more of God" is usually a euphemism for "wanting my life to go better" or "wanting nice feelings."

Delight yourself in the LORD and he will give you the desires of your heart. Be still...and wait patiently for him (Ps. 37:4,7).

I will wait for you, my God—at least I can do that.

And I will trust that You will answer (38:15). I confess my sins, and my desire to sin. These ugly realities trouble me (38:18). O Lord, do not forsake me now (38:21)!

Can You help me to want You? Can You begin this day in my heart with a gift of delight in You alone?

It is God who works in you to will and to act according to his good purpose (Phil. 2:13).

Work in me, Lord—tear down, dig up, re-create. Do Your work!

I am Your delinquent child. Some days I fight against You—I kick Your shins, I sneak around, I couldn't care less. My wrong desires keep me in a trap of my own making (Prov. 11:6). But Your name is branded on my spirit. I'm Your child—how I love that thought! Please don't turn away.

I know the plans I have for you...plans to prosper you and not to harm you, plans to give you hope and a future. Then you will call upon me and come and pray to me, and I will listen to you. You will seek me and find me when you seek me with all your heart. I will be found by you (Jer. 29:11-14).

Thank You, Lord, for Your relentless tenderness (Jer. 31:3). How precious are Your thoughts toward me, O God! How beyond counting they are (Ps. 139:17)!

I will wait and be still while You work. I will lean intently in Your direction as I watch and listen. I will arrange my doubts, my deafness, my numbness, my delinquencies, my self-centered handicaps around me today like beggars' bowls. See—they are empty and upturned and waiting.

I will wait and be still while You fill each one with Your gifts (Heb. 4:16).

Amen.

The Depth of Divine Mercy

ou must picture me alone in that room in Magdalen, night after night, feeling, whenever my mind lifted even for a second from my work, the steady, unrelenting approach of Him whom I so earnestly desired not to meet. That which I greatly feared had at last come upon me. In the Trinity Term of 1929 I gave in, and admitted that God was God, and knelt and prayed: perhaps, that night, the most dejected and reluctant convert in all England. I did not then see what is now the most shining and obvious thing; the Divine humility which will accept a convert even on such terms. The Prodigal Son at least walked home on his own feet. But who can duly adore that Love which will open the high gates to a prodigal who is brought in kicking, struggling, resentful, and darting his eyes in every direction for a chance of escape? The words *compelle intrare,* compel them to come in,…plumb the depth of Divine mercy. The hardness of God is kinder than the softness of men, and His compulsion is our liberation.

C. S. LEWIS

Gone Blank

*He has broken my teeth with gravel; he has trampled me in the dust. I
have been deprived of peace; I have forgotten what prosperity is. So I say,
"My splendor is gone and all that I had hoped from the LORD." ... Yet
this I call to mind and therefore I have hope: Because of the LORD's
great love we are not consumed, for his compassions never fail. They are
new every morning; great is your faithfulness.*

LAMENTATIONS 3:16-18,21-23

Heavenly Father,

Thank You for including Jeremiah's lament in the Bible—all of its bitter
disappointment in life and in You, all of its anger and shame, all of its
honest pain and confusion. Jerusalem had been starved into submission,
the temple looted, and Your people hauled away in chains. Surely, Jeremiah's grief expressed only a fraction of Your own.

But thank You too for Jeremiah's startling recollections of Your
goodness in the middle of all the woe:

—God's love still saves me, even out of this (v. 22).

—God's mercies still cover me, and they always will (vv. 22-23).

—God's faithfulness still gives me peace, even now (v. 23).

When my life feels mangled and left for dead, lift me above my
own pain to receive strength from You and to respond in faith to
You. How often I turn sour, start casting blame, stop trusting—all
because my memory of Your unfailing goodness has gone blank.

Father, I ask for Jeremiah's blessed recollections today.

Amen.

Because You Noticed Pennies

Jesus sat down opposite the place where the offerings were put and watched the crowd putting their money into the temple treasury. Many rich people threw in large amounts. But a poor widow came and put in two very small copper coins, worth only a fraction of a penny. Calling his disciples to him, Jesus said, "I tell you the truth, this poor widow has put more into the treasury than all the others. They all gave out of their wealth; but she, out of her poverty, put in everything—all she had to live on."

MARK 12:41-44

Dear Lord Jesus,

Because You noticed pennies going into the offering plate from a poor woman, and knew her heart and her circumstances, and were impressed with her faith…

I ask You to help me give out of my poverty today. I'd rather wait until I have everything I want and pray for. I'd rather come to You proudly with sweet lines like "Lord, I haven't committed that sin for a month" or "Lord, I'm happy to be honorary chairperson of…" or "Lord, use my beach condo any way You like."

But help me reach deep today for my pieces of copper: My time. My inconvenience. My pride. My last buck.

Bring the whole tithe into the storehouse, that there may be food in my house. Test me in this, and see if I will not throw open the floodgates of heaven and pour out so much blessing that you will not have room enough for it (Mal. 3:10).

Help me to give sacrificially, Lord, because You notice. And I'll look for Your blessing expectantly, because You are faithful and extravagant.

Amen.

Family Spirit

The Spirit gives life; the flesh counts for nothing. The words I have spoken to you are spirit and they are life.

JOHN 6:63

O Lord,

Today I pray that Your Spirit will live in my home and all those whose lives are closely linked with mine. Make us part of Your kingdom, not through rules, but through righteousness, peace, and joy in Your Holy Spirit (Rom. 14:17).

From birth, we're so stuck in "flesh" (Ps. 51:5): schedules, aches, nagging worries, pride, and our silly human way of limiting You. Give us life, O Spirit! Free us from sin and doubt and distraction. Help us to sing Your song all day. Let us pour forth—as Your other created things do—the praises of God (Ps. 8:1; 19:2).

Holy Spirit, enter here, by every door, every impulse. Yes, come in! Come in and be King!

The world cannot accept (the Spirit of truth), because it neither sees him nor knows him. But you know him, for he lives with you and will be in you (John 14:17).

Thank You, loving Lord! Let my children's every turning be toward You. Be pleased to dwell in my marriage in fullness so that my spouse and I will always be in step with You (Gal. 5:25).

Anoint all our conversations with grace. Season our humor with kindness. Nudge us to serve. Compel us to be grateful for everything.

Living Holy Spirit, enter here.

Amen.

The Wellspring

Above all else, guard your heart, for it is the wellspring of life.

PROVERBS 4:23

PRAYING FROM PROVERBS 4

Dear Lord,

A spring gushing from the rock, a river in the desert, streams of living water—this is how You describe the outpouring of new life from my reborn heart. This wellspring is Your miracle, Lord. "All my fountains are in you" (Ps. 87:7)! But how can I guard it? Teach me from Your Word:

Keep corrupt talk far from your lips (Prov. 4:24). Profanity, gossip, vulgarity, criticism, and sarcasm seem to define the vocabulary of our times. But not of Your people (Eph. 5:4-6). Show me in a fresh way today the power of a word (James 3:1-12). Put a guard on my tongue. May all my words be pleasing in Your sight, O Lord (Ps. 19:14).

Let your eyes look straight ahead (Prov. 4:25). Help me guard my desires, loyalties, impulses, and spending habits. I place every one of these in Your ownership today (1 Pet. 3:15). Help me "train my brain" to the kind of single-mindedness that gets results (James 1:5-8).

Take only ways that are firm (Prov. 4:26). Temptation and irresponsibility can look exciting at the outset. But they turn into dead ends. No matter how smart or mature I think I am, help me choose proven paths today—of honesty, integrity, humility, and hard work. God's truths can save me from endless waste and pain (James 3:13-17).

You are the Lord, the spring of living water (Jer. 17:13). Spring up in me today. Yes, drench me and others with Your beauty and life!

Amen.

Breaking the Strongholds

The weapons we fight with are not the weapons of the world. On the contrary, they have divine power to demolish strongholds.

2 CORINTHIANS 10:4

PRAYING FROM EPHESIANS 6

Lord,

Today I pray that you would equip me for spiritual battles.

Help me to put on your full armor, so that when the day of evil comes, I will be able to stand my ground, and after I've done all I can do, I'll be able to keep standing (v. 13).

Show me how to buckle the belt of truth around my waist, and how to fasten the breastplate of righteousness in place (v. 14). May I speak truthfully, Lord, and may I say what is right. Help me to treasure integrity.

Fit my feet with the readiness that comes from the gospel of peace (v. 15). May I be as eager to spread your good news as a Nike-clad runner at the starting line!

Give me strength to take up the shield of faith, with which I can extinguish all the flaming arrows of the evil one (v. 16). May I be so full of faith that when Satan tries to bring doubt or fear, he is doused by my steady trust in You!

How I thank You, Father, for my helmet of salvation, which protects me from ultimate death. May I continually take up the sword of the Spirit, which is your Word (v. 17). And after I am fully clothed with your armor, help me to stay alert and pray (v. 18).

Amen.

Low Rung on a Rickety Ladder

Don't let anyone look down on you because you are young, but set an example for the believers in speech, in life, in love, in faith and in purity.

1 TIMOTHY 4:12

Loving Father,

Thank You for the fatherly advice of Paul for Timothy, his "true son in the faith" (1 Tim. 1:2). Today I pray with Paul for those times in my life when I find myself starting at the bottom and the climb to the top seems unsure or unsafe. Teach me from Paul's loving counsel.

Help me to celebrate youthful beginnings instead of being overly intimidated by everyone else's experience. Even when I'm an apprentice, may I set an example for both my coworkers and my superiors in speech, in life, in love, in faith, and in purity (4:12).

Use these challenging times to impress on me the value of spiritual health—it lasts so much longer than outward appearances. May I become convinced that the Christian life well-lived promises great benefit, not just in eternity, but today (4:8).

When I'm most vulnerable or prone to impatience, protect me from moral and sexual compromises. Help me to always highly prize a clean conscience (5:22; 1:19). I do want to honor Your Name, Lord. Help me see through—and reject—fads or popular beliefs that don't acknowledge You (4:7).

Thank You, loving Father, that You see me as the apple of Your eye—no matter what my place on the ladder or pay scale (Ps. 17:8). Help me not to be so anxious for the future that I miss Your gifts today.

In Jesus' name I pray. Amen.

Say, "Aaahh..."

Open wide your mouth and I will fill it.

PSALM 81:10

Lord,

I open my mouth—aah, Lord, aaahh…
You are my Lord, my source, my need.
    I open for You.

The way, the truth, and the life are Yours, I declare (John 14:6).
All is well that is Yours, I declare! All is very well (Ps. 104:28)!
    I open for You.

Rise up, Holy Spirit, rise! Fill me all through—
    With power (Acts 1:8)
    And insight (Rom. 15:14)
    And Your righteousness (Phil. 1:11)
    And Your very words (Luke 21:15)
    And with the indescribable beauty of Your presence (Ps. 27:4)

I am Yours, Lord.
    Today I open for You alone.
    Aaahh…!

Nothing Less

God, of your goodness, give me yourself; for you are sufficient for me. I cannot properly ask anything less, to be worthy of you. If I were to ask less, I should always be in want. In you alone do I have all.

JULIAN OF NORWICH

7 x Praise = Peace

Seven times a day I praise you for your righteous laws. Great peace have they who love your law, and nothing can make them stumble.

PSALM 119:164-165

Great and Wonderful God,

When I get up, I will praise You for Your creative powers, for new beginnings and for another day of life. "This is the day the LORD has made; let us rejoice and be glad in it" (Ps. 118:24).

When I have breakfast, I will praise You for daily provisions for my family's needs—like food, shelter, and money. "You open your hand and satisfy the desires of every living thing" (Ps. 145:16).

When I start work or school, I will praise You for meaningful tasks I can put my whole heart into. "That everyone may eat and drink, and find satisfaction in all his toil—this is the gift of God" (Eccles. 3:13).

When I pause for lunch, I will praise You for health and strength. "The God of Israel gives power and strength to his people" (Ps. 68:35).

When I'm worn out at the end of the day, I will praise You for my limitations. "But he said to me, 'My grace is sufficient for you, for my power is made perfect in weakness'" (2 Cor. 12:9).

When I'm enjoying dinner, I'll praise You for family and friends. "Blessed are all who fear the LORD, who walk in his ways" (Ps. 128:1).

When I go to bed, I will praise You for Your gifts of peace, comfort, and rest. "My people will live in peaceful dwelling places, in secure homes, in undisturbed places of rest" (Isa. 32:18).

You are worthy of praise, O Lord, and You bless Your people with peace (Ps. 29:11).

Amen.

Skinned Knuckles

[Jesus] said to Simon, "Put out into deep water, and let down the nets for a catch." Simon answered, "Master, we've worked hard all night and haven't caught anything. But because you say so, I will let down the nets."

LUKE 5:4-5

PRAYING FROM LUKE 5

Lord Jesus,

You ask me to push off from the shore today, out to deep water. There I will find what You have for me. How can that be? I was just out there, and all I got was wet and tired.

You see my skinned knuckles, aching back, and empty boat. But Lord, I will say this: Thank You for being here, for knowing each need, every disappointment.

Teach me obedience, Master, as you did those half-soaked fishermen, those hungry wives, those wide-eyed kids. They wanted food and health and safety—the usual requirements. You gave them that and more—"the good news of the kingdom of God," because that is why You were sent (Luke 4:43).

By faith, Lord, I put out into deep water. Forgive me for quitting too soon. Show me where to go today, what to do. I'll leave the safe and the known behind today, if You'll go with me.

I will let down the nets for a catch. What are my nets doing in the boat anyway? Maybe my talents, my attentions, the tools of my trade as Your disciple are lying around unused. Maybe I just need to try again. Lord, by faith I expect You to fill my nets.

"Don't be afraid," you said (Luke 5:10). How often You've been limited by my feelings, my cautiousness, my personal perspective, and the faithless decisions that seem to grow out of all that. It's just self-centeredness, Lord. Forgive me for fears that limit Your ability to act on my behalf.

You said, "From now on you will catch men" (v. 10). Yes, Lord, whatever You put me on earth to do—that is the measure of my real success. Empower me to do Your work. I want the "big catch" You have in mind today.

Today, Lord, I give you my silly boat, my skinned knuckles, my bad luck at fishing. Use or don't use them as You wish. By Your grace and strength, I will do what You say, and follow You (v. 11).

Amen.

Where Miracles Begin

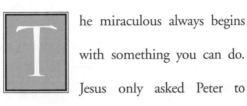he miraculous always begins with something you can do. Jesus only asked Peter to "launch out." He didn't ask him to produce the catch. But often the miraculous also begins with something you don't want to do. It requires time, energy, or resources that you'd rather not expend. It's all about fishing where you've already fished—just because He asks you to.

ROY HICKS JR.

Night Stalker

Who of you by worrying can add a single hour to his life?

MATTHEW 6:27

PRAYING FROM MATTHEW 6

Lord Jesus,

Worry is a night stalker at my house. When I'm leaning over bills by lamplight, listening to sirens go by, or drifting off to sleep, Worry walks in. And he's always followed by cold drafts of doubt and misery. Soon I'm behaving in ways I hate: gnawing away on new threats or old fears, replaying doom-and-gloom scenarios, trying to fix unfixable things in my life…

Do not worry about your life, what you will eat or drink; or about your body, what you will wear (v. 25).

Lord Jesus, forgive me. Help me. I've given You my today and my tomorrows, my joys and my dreads—why do I let Worry suck me into his obsessions? Do I doubt Your love or Your power?

God clothes the grass of the field.… Will he not much more clothe you, O you of little faith? (v. 30).

Lord, grant me a liberating confidence in You today that will empower me to push ahead through the ever-present unknowns, out-of-my-control situations, and always-possible disasters. Show me simple steps I can take to be wise and careful—and help me to take them, not just worry about them! Yet may the untidy realities of this world never rob me of the wonders You're trying to accomplish through my life today.

So do not worry, saying, "What shall we eat?" or "What shall we drink?" or "What shall we wear?" For...your heavenly Father knows that you need them. But seek first his kingdom and his righteousness, and all these things will be given to you as well (vv. 31-33).

Thank You, Lord. With Your help I'll padlock the doors and windows against Worry tonight. Please, Lord, free me from this unwelcome specter in my life.

Ask and you will receive, and your joy will be complete (John 16:24).

I do ask today, Lord. I ask, I surrender, I gird myself with faith in You. By Your Spirit, bring these powerful truths to mind day or night. May Your words of guarantee be the locks guarding my peace when Worry tries to slide back in.

Do not be terrified; do not be discouraged, for the LORD your God will be with you wherever you go (Josh. 1:9).

Cast all your anxiety on him because he cares for you (1 Pet. 5:7).

I will lie down and sleep in peace, for you alone, O LORD, make me dwell in safety (Ps. 4:8).

Thank You, Lord of peace and safety.

Amen.

The Truth About Father

There is but one God, the Father, from whom all things came and for whom we live.

1 CORINTHIANS 8:6

MEDITATIONS FOR YOUR DAY

I am surrounded by my Father's favor like a shield.
(Ps. 5:12)

I'm always on His mind.
(Psalm 139)

When the way gets long, my Father carries me.
(Deut. 1:29-31)

I am always welcome in my Father's presence.
(Heb. 10:19-22)

When I leave, I break my Father's heart.
(Hosea 11)

He would die for me.
(John 3:16)

Jesus came to show me how my Father wants me to live.
(John 14:6-7)

I can always, always count on my Father's love.
(Rom. 8:38-39)

One Plus One

"For this reason a man will leave his father and mother and be united to his wife, and the two will become one flesh." So they are no longer two, but one.

MATTHEW 19:5-6

Lord of married lovers,
Only you could defy the law of mathematics to make one plus one equal one. And that "one" is not even two halves that add up to a whole but two drastically different people who add up to an entirely new creation: Us!

We come before you in prayer on behalf of Us—a husband and wife who long to reflect Your beautiful likeness (Gen. 5:2) and experience the amazing oneness You promise: "Has not the LORD made them one? In flesh and spirit they are his" (Mal. 2:15).

Yet, You hear the voices, Lord, that attempt to separate Us: "Are you sure you did the right thing?" "You deserve more than this." "What if you get bored?" "Well, as long as you're happy…"

But You've shown Us "the most excellent way" (1 Cor. 12:31)—cherishing our commitment as we cleave to one another (Gen. 2:24), nurturing mutual respect as we submit to each other (Eph. 5:21), finding our lives as we surrender them to You (Luke 9:24).

And this way of love will never fail (1 Cor. 13:8).

Lord of married lovers, bind Us together in an everlasting covenant. We dedicate Us to You.

Amen.

Name Above All Names

The throne of God and of the Lamb will be in the city, and his servants will serve him. They will see his face, and his name will be on their foreheads.

REVELATION 22:3-4

Dear Lord God,

I kneel before You, Father. Yes, Father! Your whole creation family derives our name—"children of God"—from that name (Eph. 3:14-15; 1 John 3:1). Your name is unknowable, sacred, powerful, and so important to You. Hallowed be Your name (Isa. 57:15; Prov. 18:10; Matt. 6:9).

You are Wonderful Counselor. Your wisdom made the world, yet it is available to give me guidance and solve tough problems (Jer. 51:15; James 3:17). Thank You. Today when I hear Your voice whispering, "This is the way, walk in it," help me to obey (1 Kings 19:12; Heb. 3:15).

You are Mighty God. "Who is like you—majestic in holiness, awesome in glory, working wonders?" (Exod. 15:11). Nothing is too hard for You, and You never get tired (Jer. 32:17; Isa. 40:28). You are the only power worthy of worship—and I do praise You.

You are Everlasting Father. By Christ's tender intervention, You have adopted me into Your family and made me an heir of heaven (Gal. 4:6-7). How great is the love that You've lavished on me, Father, that I should be called "child of God" (1 John 3:1).

You are Prince of Peace. Your very presence brings peace to Your people, our home, and my heart. When serious need, opposition, illness, even death threaten, I can dwell in the green pastures of peace and provision (Psalm 23). How deep and mysterious, yet strong and enduring is this peace of heaven You offer (Phil. 4:6-7; John 14:27)! Thank You.

For all that You are, I praise You, I worship You, Lord. May Your name and Your reputation be honored by my words, thoughts, and activities today (1 Tim. 6:1).

Amen.

Because You Wept

When Mary reached the place where Jesus was and saw him, she fell at his feet and said, "Lord, if you had been here, my brother [Lazarus] would not have died." When Jesus saw her weeping, and the Jews who had come along with her also weeping, he was deeply moved in spirit and troubled. "Where have you laid him?" he asked. "Come and see, Lord," they replied. Jesus wept. Then the Jews said, "See how he loved him!"

JOHN 11:32-36

Dear Lord Jesus,

Because You wept with Your friends when they wept, and held Lazarus and his sisters in such deep affection (John 11:5), and because You allowed Your God-heart to be pierced by loss and dread of death...

I ask You, by this same kindness—give me a compassionate heart today. Break through that shiny exterior of easy platitudes that keeps me safe from others' griefs. "Rejoice with those who rejoice;" Your Word says, "mourn with those who mourn" (Rom. 12:15).

Whose emotion or circumstance do You want me to share (affirm, listen to, be touched by, help carry, or celebrate) today? Open my eyes to the person—even very close to me—to whom I've become blind or uncaring. Your tears show me a better way to live.

Carry each other's burdens, and in this way you will fulfill the law of Christ (Gal. 6:2).

Lord, thank You for caring. Help me to care too.

Amen.

Does God Watch Peter Jennings?

The groans of the dying rise from the city, and the souls of the wounded cry out for help. But God charges no one with wrongdoing.

JOB 24:12

Lord,

Are You watching Peter Jennings?

Almost every day I see terrible news on TV—genocide, persecution and torture, robberies and rapes, random violence, even the slaughter of innocent women and children.

Today I pray for understanding and for faith when I don't understand. At times, I cry out with Jeremiah, "Why do the wicked prosper? Why do the ones without faith live at ease?" (from Jer. 12:1). With the writer of Ecclesiastes, I say, "I have thought deeply about all that goes on here in the world, where people have the power of injuring each other" (Eccles. 8:9, TLB).

Hear my questions, mysterious Lord:

Since You are love (1 John 4:7-9), why do You let the innocent suffer?

Since You are just and fair (Deut. 32:4), why don't You step in to bring scammers, abusers, philanderers, thieves, and despots to justice?

Since You are good and merciful to all (Nah. 1:7; 2 Pet. 3:9), why do You let beautiful children die orphaned, starving, and alone?

Since You have the power to accomplish anything (Jer. 32:17), why don't You prevent natural disasters, avert car wrecks that kill happy prom nighters, and keep young, working dads from getting multiple sclerosis?

Thank You for hearing me out, for inviting me to go ahead and ask these painful questions. Remind me, Father, of the truths I do know.

Help me persist in areas where You want to reveal important, difficult lessons. Pry my fingers away from the questions that lead nowhere but to bitterness and doubt.

I do know some things about You, Lord, and I'm building my hopes on them:

—I believe that You are strong and loving, even when I can't explain (Ps. 62:11-12; 18:30).

—I know that You care for your own (Psalm 23).

—I believe that You are ultimately in control (Ps. 146:10).

—I trust that You will bring the wicked to justice and comfort the oppressed (Jer. 9:24).

This is my prayer then: May I feel angry when I see all the evil under the sun. But let my outrage be directed at the source of evil—man's sin and Satan's schemes—and not at You. Your Word assures me that You cannot even be tempted by evil, Father. Man sins. But You only give good gifts to man (James 1:13-18).

Rather than despairing over evil, I pray that as I watch the evening news, a passion will ignite in my heart to do everything I can to bring Your love, justice, and salvation to this suffering world. Jesus taught us to pray "Your will be done on earth as it is in heaven" (Matt. 6:10). And I am one agent of Your will in this world. I touch with Your hands; I go with Your feet. Forgive me, Father, for how often I conveniently forget this.

I know that dreary network news will always be with us, Lord. But today I pray that I and many others of Your followers would become part of Isaiah's Good News network: *How beautiful on the mountains are the feet of those who bring good news, who proclaim peace, who bring good tidings, who proclaim salvation, who say to Zion, "Your God reigns!"* (Isa. 52:7).

Amen.

Suffering Toward God

very truth about suffering can be twisted into a weapon for or against God. Most often suffering speeds us in the direction we are already heading—whether toward or away from God.

DAVID McKENNA

Free Indeed

It is for freedom that Christ has set us free. Stand firm, then, and do not let yourselves be burdened again by a yoke of slavery.

GALATIANS 5:1

Lord Jesus Christ,

I pray today that You will release me from any spiritual powers that may be holding me captive. I don't pray with any power of my own; only You can save and liberate (1 John 4:14). Only You are greater than Satan or any authority or influence in this world (Jude 9; 1 John 4:4). You have disarmed all the powers of evil and "made a public spectacle of them, triumphing over them by the cross" (Col. 2:15). And You are stronger than any addiction, habit, dependency, or destructive pull in my life (Ps. 103:3-4; Matt. 18:18).

In Your name and by the power of Your costly shed blood, please rescue me from any dark powers that I've allowed to influence me or my family, and bring us safely into Your kingdom of light (Phil. 2:9-11; Heb. 9:11-14; Col. 1:13). Especially break down the strongholds that I don't see—like bitterness, spiritual blindness, immorality, or fear (2 Cor. 10:3-4; Heb. 12:15; 2 Cor. 4:4; 1 Cor. 6:9-10; Rom. 8:15). Keep me from thoughtlessly sliding back into bondage (Gal. 5:1,19-21).

I thank You and worship You right now in faith for the deliverances and new beginnings You have brought, are bringing, and will yet bring. And as You deliver me, take up residence in my heart, filling every corner (Luke 11:21-26). Where there used to be sin, may Your Holy Spirit bring the beautiful fruit of love, joy, peace, patience, kindness, goodness, faithfulness, gentleness, and self-control (Gal. 5:22).

Amen.

Right Before My Eyes

*Do not be terrified.... The LORD your God, who is going before you,
will fight for you, as he did for you in Egypt, before your very eyes, and
in the desert. There you saw how the LORD your God carried you, as a
father carries his son, all the way you went until you reached this place.*

DEUTERONOMY 1:29-31

Heavenly Father,

So often You reassured Your people by reminding them about what
You'd already accomplished for them in the past. Thank You for
reminding them, and me, "Remember that time? I saved you right
before your eyes!"

Today, I call to mind a time when You went before me in an uncer-
tain situation: _____. Even as troubles were closing in, You
opened up a way for me. Thank You, Lord.

Today, I will remember a time and place when You fought for me
(before my very eyes!): _____. All my strength was gone,
and I was up against an enemy that seemed so impossible to conquer.

Today, I will remind my spirit of a time when You picked me up
and gently carried me, just like You carried the Israelites so long ago:
_____. I was like a lost child in Your arms, unable to go on.

Today, I thank You that I can go into my tomorrows with hope
because of all You have already done for me. With the psalmist I can
say, "I trust in your unfailing love; my heart rejoices in your salvation. I
will sing to the LORD, for he has been good to me" (Ps. 13:5-6).

I remember You, tremendous Lord—and my eyes are open!
Amen.

Breakfast on the Beach

*When [the disciples] landed, they saw a fire of burning coals there with fish
on it, and some bread.… Jesus said to them, "Come and have breakfast."
None of the disciples dared ask him, "Who are you?" They knew it was the
Lord. Jesus came, took the bread and gave it to them, and did the same
with the fish. This was now the third time Jesus appeared to his disciples
after he was raised from the dead. When they had finished eating, Jesus said
to Simon Peter, "Simon son of John, do you truly love me more than these?"
"Yes, Lord," he said, "you know that I love you."*

JOHN 21:9,12-15

Dear Lord Jesus,
Because You made breakfast on the beach to show that You had truly,
physically come back from the dead (and missed Your friends); because
You wanted to show Your love tangibly to hungry men; because You came
back to tenderly lead Peter through his painful confession to restoration…

I pray that I'll always respond to Your grace when I fail. You're so
much more powerful than my amazing knack for flubbing badly. When
that happens, help me humble myself under Your mighty hand, that
You may lift me up in due time (1 Pet. 5:6). With Peter I exclaim today,
"Praise be to the God and Father of our Lord Jesus Christ! In his great
mercy he has given us new birth into a living hope" (1 Pet. 1:3).

Show me today how to live exuberantly in Your extravagant grace.
Help me celebrate it with those who know You, and demonstrate it to
those who still don't have a clue. All day, I want to hear that crackling
fire, smell breakfast cooking, and hear the risen Lord of Grace laughing
with His friends.

Amen.

Amazing Grace!

Grace and truth came through Jesus Christ.

JOHN 1:17

MEDITATIONS FOR YOUR DAY

Having been justified by Your grace,
I have become an heir of God
having the hope of eternal life.
(Titus 3:7)

In You I have redemption through Christ's blood, the forgiveness of sins,
in accordance with the riches of Your grace that You lavished on me
with all wisdom and understanding.
(Eph. 1:7-8)

Your grace is sufficient for me,
because Your power is made perfect in my weakness.
(2 Cor. 12:9)

Prayer for a Daughter

I am sending you out like sheep among wolves. Therefore be as shrewd as
snakes and as innocent as doves.

MATTHEW 10:16

Lord,

You've blessed my daughter _____ with a sweet, guileless, and
giving nature. What a gift she is to our family!

She's a tender lamb, a harmless dove, but look at the world we're in,
Lord Jesus! My prayer today is that You would keep her spirit from hurt
and harm. Mature her so that her tenderness doesn't render her gullible
or foolish (Hos. 7:11). Underneath her sweet exterior, make her astute
and perceptive (Matt. 10:16).

Bless her with a beautiful strength, a wise innocence, a shielded vul-
nerability (1 Pet. 3:4-5). How much you could nurture, heal, comfort,
and encourage others through such gifts, Lord!

Bring her a husband in your time who will cherish her, honor her,
and protect her for exactly these wonderful qualities.

For her whole life, I claim these truths for her from Psalm 91:

You will be her true dwelling place and refuge (vv. 1-2); under Your
wings she will find covering and comfort (v. 4); You will save her from
terrors and fears (v. 5);You will protect her from physical and spiritual
diseases (v. 6); You will give Your angels power to guard her (vv. 11-13);
You will answer her when she calls, because You love her (v. 15).

Yes, Lord, You will always treasure her even more than I do. I thank
You and bless You!

Amen.

Prayer for a Son

I am sending to you Timothy, my son whom I love.

1 CORINTHIANS 4:17

Holy, Living Father,
I join with the apostle Paul today in earnest prayer for my son,

_____.

Teach him how to enjoy his youth, without worrying if others look down on him because he's still learning. Even now, may he set an example for others in speech, in life, in love, in faith, and in purity (1 Tim. 4:12).

Help him value godliness more than fitness or appearance. May he learn that godliness holds promise for both the present life and the life to come (4:8). Show him how to keep himself pure (5:22), highly prizing a clean conscience (1:19).

I pray that he would see through—and reject—godless myths and fads, no matter how popular or how many of his peers embrace them (4:7). Help him to pursue more than money with his talents; may he pursue instead the wealth that comes from righteousness, godliness, faith, love, endurance, and gentleness (6:11).

In Your time, bring him a wife who will cherish him and honor the gifts You've placed in him (2 Tim. 1:6). Thank You that he can approach his future without fear, because You've given him the "spirit of power, of love and of self-discipline" (1:7). May he love Your word, that is able to make him wise (3:15).

Help my son, Father, to fight the good fight of faith his whole life. May he treasure and celebrate the eternal destiny to which he was called when he confessed You as Lord (1 Tim. 6:12).

Amen.

On Days Like This

Why are you downcast, O my soul? Why so disturbed within me?
Put your hope in God, for I will yet praise him, my Savior and my God.

PSALM 42:11

Lord Jesus,

It's a downcast day—bleak feelings, heavy thoughts, a drizzle of discouragement in myself and in those I live and work with. For all of us, I lift these dreary thoughts and feelings to you, Light of the World. I know You care (1 Pet. 5:7).

Don't let your heart be troubled. Trust in me (from John 14:1).

Lord, You understand these drizzle days. As a child, You endured drab days. As a man, You held on through anguish and tears. You were made like us in every way so that You could become our merciful and faithful high priest (Heb. 2:17).

Don't let your happy trust in me die away, no matter what is happening. Remember your reward (from Heb. 10:35, TLB).

How I thank You, Lord, that on days just like this, You take our burdens on Yourself so we don't have to carry them (Matt. 11:28). Thank You that no matter how unappealing our emotions are, You're always at work, renewing us day by day (2 Cor. 4:16). Renew me, Lord.

I am the God of hope. Let me fill you with joy and peace so that you may overflow with the power of my Holy Spirit (from Rom. 15:13).

Lord, because of who You are, today can be a good day. I trust You.

My redeemed one, soon you will be singing! (from Isa. 51:11).

Amen.

Tracks in the Outback

From the ends of the earth I call to you, I call as my heart grows faint.

PSALM 61:2

PRAYING WITH DAVID IN THE WILDERNESS

Lord,

Here I am again in the outback. I think I'm supposed to be here, and I know You're here with me. But where to now? Did I miss a turn, a trail marker, a road to somewhere else? I'm so capable of dumb mistakes.

Every move matters now. Every pro and con. But I've never felt more scattered, doubtful, in the dark.

I am with you to deliver you (Jer. 1:8, NASB).

Should I try to follow my tracks out, find a way back to someplace that makes sense?

Look straight ahead. Do not turn to the right or the left (from Prov. 4:27).

You promised a good future (Ps. 112:1-2), safety (Ps. 121:7-8), the comforts of home (Psalm 128), honor among peers (Ps. 112:9), and light "even in darkness" (Ps. 112:4). Were You talking to someone else?

I know the plans I have for you, plans to prosper you and not to harm you. No eye has seen, no ear has heard, no mind has conceived what I have prepared for those who love Me (from Jer. 29:11; 1 Cor. 2:9).

In this wilderness, I reach for You today. Teach me from the prayers of David during his trackless years in the desert, when everywhere he looked he saw only hunger and danger and dust. All he had to go on were Your promises.

You, O LORD, keep my lamp burning; my God turns my darkness into light (Ps. 18:28).

Yes, Lord, You are my source of understanding and hope, no matter how in the dark I am.

He guides the humble in what is right and teaches them his way (Ps. 25:9).

Yes, Lord, You will guide me forward step by step if I keep looking to You and honoring You as Lord. I don't have to know the way!

I am still confident of this: I will see the goodness of the LORD in the land of the living (Ps 27:13).

Yes, Lord, I believe in good things ahead. I trust You.

O my Strength, I watch for you;... God will go before me (Ps. 59:9-10).

Yes, Lord, I watch and wait and listen. Help me to take this confidence with me into my day: that You are going before me in every choice, every risky situation, every exciting opportunity—and every confusion, too. You are worthy of my worship today.

Amen.

Step by Step

God guides us, despite our uncertainties and our vagueness, even through our failings and mistakes. He often starts us off to the left, only to bring us up in the end to the right; or else he brings us back to the right, after a long detour, because we started off by mistake to the left in the belief that we were obeying him. He leads us step by step, from event to event. Only afterwards, as we look back over the way we have come and reconsider certain important moments in our lives in the light of all that has followed them, or when we survey the whole progress of our lives, do we experience the feeling of having been led without knowing it, the feeling that God has mysteriously guided us.

PAUL TOURNIER

What the Lover Said

He has clothed me with garments of salvation and draped about me the robe of righteousness. I am like a bridegroom in his wedding suit or a bride with her jewels.

ISAIAH 61:10, TLB

Lord, lover of heaven,
How can You bear to look at me? I am a walking ruin, a casualty of the sin defect—and I live among others just like me. An awful fate looms (Isa. 6:5)! Surely I have been damaged and ugly from birth (Ps. 51:5).

Why would You write a Bible for me? When I consider Your beautiful world—the work of your fingers, the moon and the stars You have set in place—I can't help wondering why You'd even care about someone like me (Ps. 8:3-4).

How beautiful you are, my darling! Oh, how beautiful! To me, you are like a lily among thorns (from Song of Songs 1:15; 2:2).

I will keep you for Myself like a dove in the clefts of the rock, in the hiding places on the mountainside. Show me your face, My loved one. Let me hear your voice all day. Your voice is sweet, and your face is lovely (from 2:14).

This is the heritage of My loved ones—your righteousness is of Me (from Isa. 54:17, KJV). *I have become Your beauty, holiness, and redemption* (from 1 Cor. 1:30).

Praise to the End

Praise the LORD, O my soul; all my inmost being, praise his holy name.
Praise the LORD, O my soul, and forget not all his benefits.

PSALM 103:1-2

PRAYING PSALM 103

Praise the Lord!

Yes, I praise You, God, with every part of my being! Emotions, will, mind, body, soul, and spirit—all praise You (v. 1)! You are flawless!

I exalt You today and give You all my worship because You are good, and what You are accomplishing in my life is a miracle (v. 2).

You have forgiven my sins, freed me from my past, and covered me with Jesus' own righteousness and grace. And every day as I confess my failings to You, You forgive me again and again and bury my sins in the deep end of the ocean (vv. 3,12; 1 John 1:9). Thank You, Lord!

You give me healing in body, mind, and spirit. You remove my infirmities and hold me up in my sorrows. By Your wounds, You make me whole (Isa. 53:4; 1 Pet. 2:24). I praise You with every cell and nerve ending in my body!

Every day in ways I don't even see, You spare me from the grave (Ps. 107:20). You've rescued me from a future in hell. As You rose from death, Lord Jesus, I will too! (Ps. 103:4; Mal. 4:2). Thank You!

You surround my life each day with evidences of Your compassion—they spread over me like a night sky full of stars; they lay all around me like a field of diamonds. Your love carries me on the strongest wings. Honestly, some days I seem to soar (103:5)! All praise to You, Lord God!

Even in this broken world, You are at work bringing justice and hope for the oppressed, guiding those who seek Your wisdom, and lavishing Your mercies and trustworthiness on everyone (vv. 6-8).

You remember our limits, our foolishness, the wilt that sets in so soon on every bloom of human triumph, and still You love us. Your love is a good Father's love—passionate, constant, and tender. From eternity past to eternity future, Your love for us is guaranteed (vv. 13-17).

With the angels today I praise You, great God! (Praise is my reason for being.) With every created thing, I acknowledge You as King.

Praise from the beginning!

Praise to the end!

Praise the Lord, O my soul (v. 22).

Amen.

Actively Waiting

Be still before the LORD and wait patiently for him; do not fret.

PSALM 37:7

Dear Lord,

I'm a grade-schooler in Your presence today—fidgety, distracted, interrupting, anxious.

Do not fret. Fretting is so unbecoming to a kingdom child. Only self-centered, problem-focused, small-thinking spirits fret. (Forgive me, Lord.) *Do not,* because it's a simple choice, a critical shift of viewpoint. Just *do not fret,* otherwise I'll never see Your face or notice Your answers or experience Your miracles today.

Wait patiently. Wait. Don't leave, don't do, don't talk or argue or ask. (Is waiting another word for worship?) *Patiently*—giving up my own opinions of what's a good use of my time; laying aside my brittle requirements of how and when You, God of this conversation, should respond. Just *wait patiently,* because nothing else is so worthy of my time.

Be still. I want to be still before You. Help me to learn stillness. To turn off all those buzzy preoccupations (is preoccupation another word for idol?), and to bear with stillness in Your presence. The stillness of respect…surrender…receptivity, because no other voice but Yours means life to me.

Wait on Me. In due season, I will honor you with every blessing (from Ps. 37:34, TLB).

In this stillness, I wait, Sovereign God. It is good to wait quietly for You (Lam. 3:26).

Amen.

Wait in Stillness

Do not be afraid of silence in your prayer time. It may be that you are meant to listen, not to speak. So wait before the Lord. Wait in stillness. Wait as David waited when he "sat before the Lord." And in that stillness, assurance will come to you. You will know that you are heard; you will know that your Lord ponders the voice of your humble desires; you will hear quiet words spoken to you yourself, perhaps to your grateful surprise and refreshment.

AMY CARMICHAEL

Crisis Management

Some men came and told [King] Jehoshaphat, "A vast army is coming against you from Edom...." Alarmed, Jehoshaphat resolved to inquire of the LORD, and he proclaimed a fast for all Judah.... Then Jehoshaphat stood up in the assembly...and said: "O LORD, God of our fathers,...we will stand in your presence...and will cry out to you in our distress, and you will hear us and save us.... We have no power to face this vast army.... We do not know what to do, but our eyes are upon you."... Then the Spirit of the LORD came upon Jahaziel.... He said: "The battle is not yours, but God's.... Take up your positions; stand firm and see the deliverance the LORD will give you...." Early in the morning...Jehoshaphat appointed men to sing to the LORD and to praise him for the splendor of his holiness as they went out at the head of the army, saying: "Give thanks to the LORD, for his love endures forever."

2 CHRONICLES 20:2-21

Heavenly Father,

Help me to learn from Jehoshaphat's crisis-management plan: He took his concerns to You first; he nurtured morale for those in his care; he led by example; he acknowledged that he didn't have all the answers; he listened to guidance; and he armed his people with praise.

Why not? The situation might be grave, but God had promised victory. O, let me sing like that, especially when I face challenges today that only You can handle! The battle is Yours, not mine, and Your love endures forever. Father, I ask for Jehoshaphat's bold (slightly crazy) trust.

Amen.

Talented and Gifted

Each one should use whatever gift he has received to serve others,
faithfully administering God's grace in its various forms.

1 PETER 4:10

Lord,

You made me on purpose, with divine genius, as an expression of Your
joy (Ps. 139:13-15; Gen. 1:31). How awesome are Your creative ways
and Your loving intentions for me! How priceless is Your every thought
in my direction (Ps. 139:17).

But today I wonder, What do You have in mind? How can I
express Your creation miracle? Show me, wonderful Counselor
(Isa. 28:29).

By Your Spirit of truth, lead me clearly to uncover and develop
those interests and abilities that add up to "me." Grant me the commitment to make the most of these gifts—to practice, learn, and train with
diligence. Give me Your grace when those around me don't understand
or affirm my differences.

Reveal also those spiritual gifts You've granted me to build up the
community of believers—gifts like teaching, service, comforting others,
and healing (1 Cor. 12:7-10; Rom. 12:6-8). I dedicate these, wholly
and holy, to You.

Yes, plant in me a lifelong desire to use any talent—be it physical,
mental, or spiritual—to serve You (1 Cor. 12:4-11). And with those
around me today, may I be an encourager like Paul, who urged Timothy, "Don't neglect the gift God has given you!" (from 1 Tim. 4:14).

Amen.

Life 101

He has showed you, O man, what is good. And what does the LORD require of you? To act justly and to love mercy and to walk humbly with your God.

MICAH 6:8

Father,

Everyone seems to have a different plan for success: get mean, or go with the flow; swim with the sharks, or soar with the "goddess"; dress for success, or live to excess; get in touch with your inner child, or get in touch with a good accountant…

Help me sort through the cacophony of advice, Lord. Help me learn from the best and ignore the rest. And grant me Your wisdom to know the difference.

Today, Lord, help me to shape my desires and activities around the "Life 101" requirements You gave to the prophet Micah:

To act justly. Teach me to be fair, to give credit where it's due, and to defend those in need.

To love mercy. Teach me the meaning of compassion and grace, and show me how to extend it to others.

To walk humbly with my God. Teach me to lay aside my selfishness, pride, and arrogance. May I see myself as You do, Lord. And help me to be consciously *with* You every moment.

Today I want to reflect on these basics all day long. May they become so much a part of who I am that others will use these phrases to describe me. Now that would be true success in life!

I pray for these things in Your Name, Father, and I ask for Your strength and grace to accomplish them.

Amen.

Making Amends

When a man or woman wrongs another in any way and so is unfaithful to the LORD, that person is guilty and must confess the sin he has committed. He must make full restitution for his wrong, add one fifth to it and give it all to the person he has wronged.

NUMBERS 5:5-7

Lord of Grace,

How often I ask You for forgiveness—and how readily You extend it. Your mercy is a wonder! Forgive me when I take it for granted, thinking there's no cost to You. Every mercy I receive is a paid-in-full restitution—a "guilt offering" (Isa. 53:10)—bought for me by the agony of Christ (2 Cor. 5:21; 1 John 3:16). Thank You, forgiving Lord!

Forgive me for how careless I get when I've wronged another: a quick "I'm sorry"; a blithe "That's life"; an easy judgment that the offended party needs to "move on"; a convenient forgetfulness. Show me today where a relationship remains crippled because I've been unwilling to make amends. Help me know and face the truth today:

By Your Holy Spirit—*When he, the Spirit of truth, comes, he will guide you into all truth* (John 16:13).

By Your Word—*The word of God is living and active….it judges the thoughts and attitudes of the heart* (Heb. 4:12).

By the insight of wise friends—*Faithful are the wounds of a friend* (Prov. 27:6, NASB).

Rule in my heart by the law of love—to graciously treat others the way I want to be treated (Matt. 7:12). And empower me to take that next step toward a generous restitution.

Amen.

Lions' Lunch

I am in the midst of lions; I lie among ravenous beasts—men whose teeth are spears and arrows, whose tongues are sharp swords.

PSALM 57:4

Dear Lord,

Do You see the teeth marks on me, Lord? I'm surrounded by carnivores—evil people who oppose Your plans and Your people. And today may be the day when they make a meal of me.

Evil men will be cut off.... A little while, and the wicked will be no more. There is a future for the man of peace (Ps. 37:9-10,37).

My hope is You, Lord. But why should that feel like weakness? Why should I be ashamed because I don't strike back? Stand by me today.

No one whose hope is in Me will ever be put to shame, but they will be put to shame who are treacherous without excuse (from Ps. 25:3).

Lord, talk to my spirit. Teach me how You bring justice in Your time, in Your ways. Oh, please help me look into Your face and listen to Your words today.

Do not let your heart envy sinners, but always be zealous for the fear of the LORD. There is surely a future hope for you, and your hope will not be cut off (Prov. 23:17-18).

Thank You for the promise of hope, my God. I trust that You're coming to my rescue today.

And if You wonder where I am, just listen for the roaring...
Amen.

Friendship Lessons

Greater love has no one than this, that he lay down his life for his friends. You are my friends if you do what I command.... I have called you friends.

JOHN 15:13-15

Lord,

What a friend You are! Teach me today the "greater love" of true friendships that You intend mine to reflect:

—like Job, who prayed for his friends even though they hadn't been much help during his long illness (Job 42:10);

—like David and Jonathan, who were loyal to each other despite being caught by opposing political forces (1 Sam. 18:1-4);

—like Samuel and David, whose relationship of spiritual mentor/disciple helped prepare David to be king (1 Sam. 19:18-22);

—like the unnamed men who overcame great obstacles to carry their paralyzed friend to Jesus for healing (Mark 2:1-12);

—like Barnabas, who was the first to extend trust to the much-feared Saul after his conversion (Acts 9:26-27);

—like Paul's friends Mary and other women who "worked very hard in the Lord" on behalf of the early church (Rom. 16:6,12);

—like Paul's friend Onesiphorus, who cared for the apostle in prison and wasn't ashamed to be seen with him (2 Tim. 1:16).

Jesus, dear Friend of my soul, Friend of all who look to You in need—help me love at all times today (Prov. 17:17), for Your glory.

Amen.

The Best Hard Question

There is in Jerusalem near the Sheep Gate a pool, which in Aramaic is
called Bethesda.… Here a great number of disabled people used to lie—
the blind, the lame, the paralyzed. One who was there had been an
invalid for thirty-eight years. When Jesus saw him lying there and
learned that he had been in this condition for a long time, he asked him,
"Do you want to get well?"

JOHN 5:2-6

Lord Jesus,

Because You stopped to ask the best hard question—"Do you want to
get well?"—of a person who needed to get well more than anything on
earth…

I ask You to show me the questions I need to face today. (How
much time I spend whining for answers!) Help me to pose blunt,
revealing questions, especially in areas where my life seems stuck:

—"What is it I really want?"

—"What am I willing to do to make it happen?"

—"Who can help me?"

—"What is God revealing, or has He already revealed, about this?"

—"What is within my power to do today?"

—"If I keep failing in areas where I profess to want success so
badly, what is it that I might want more than success?"

The purposes of a man's heart are deep waters, but a man of under-
standing draws them out (Prov. 20:5).

Lord, grant me the best hard questions today, even if they hurt.
Amen.

He Wants to Talk

rayer starts with God. It is His idea. The desire to pray is the result of God's greater desire to talk with us. He has something to say when we feel the urge to pray. He is the initiator. The keen desire to begin and end the day with prolonged prayer is His gift. The sense of need to pray for challenges or opportunities throughout the day is because He has wisdom and insight He wants to impart.

LLOYD JOHN OGILVIE

"Speak, Lord—I'm Listening..."

Then Eli realized that the LORD was calling the boy. So Eli told Samuel, "Go and lie down, and if he calls you, say, 'Speak, LORD, for your servant is listening.'" So Samuel went and lay down in his place. The LORD came and stood there, calling as at the other times, "Samuel! Samuel!" Then Samuel said, "Speak, for your servant is listening."

1 SAMUEL 3:8-10

O Lord God,

Please call my children to You by name as you called Samuel and as You have called me (Isa. 43:1). Thank You that You promise to knock patiently on the door of each heart in this family (Rev. 3:20). Thank You that you pursue us (Ps. 139:5)! You did it for me—do the same for each of my children.

Yes, pursue them, Lord. Keep calling them—as You did with Samuel—until each child has said, "Yes, Lord, I'm listening."

Your promise of salvation is for children of all ages—in fact, for everyone who answers Your call (Acts 2:39; Rom. 10:13). Thank You for Your promise that as my children hear You and believe in You, they will pass from death to life (John 5:24)!

May I be like Eli, who encouraged Samuel to say yes to You. May I never hinder my children from responding to You (Mark 10:47-48). May I never say, "Not now, honey" or, "You're too young."

And far beyond the first "Yes, Lord!" may my children listen carefully to Your voice and answer quickly as long as they live.

In Jesus' name. Amen.

All Plans Aside

As Jesus and his disciples were on their way, he came to a village where a
woman named Martha opened her home to him. She had a sister called
Mary, who sat at the Lord's feet listening to what he said. But Martha was
distracted by all the preparations that had to be made. She came to him
and asked, "Lord, don't you care that my sister has left me to do the work by
myself? Tell her to help me!" "Martha, Martha," the Lord answered, "you
are worried and upset about many things, but only one thing is needed.
Mary has chosen what is better, and it will not be taken away from her."

LUKE 10:38-42

Heavenly Father,
I know Martha very well, and I'm on her side in this little argument.
She'd heard that the Master was coming, though not with time enough
to shop or clean or get things right for God Himself to stop by. She
wanted so much for things to be right—actually, perfect. And, of
course, someone's got to think ahead, take care of details, see that everyone else is happy.

But all Martha's loving, caring effort was coming to nothing
because Mary just sat there like a lump, looking holier-than-thou…and
Jesus didn't seem to notice.

Why didn't Jesus step in to settle this sibling quarrel fairly? *Only one*
thing is needed.

What was Martha doing wrong? *Choose what is better.*

(When Jesus said, "Martha, Martha," was He scolding or smiling?)

Father, teach me by Martha's complaint today. I'm putting aside all
my perfect plans. I'm sitting at Jesus' feet. I'm looking into His lovely face.
Amen.

Without Partiality

If you show special attention to the man wearing fine clothes and say, "Here's a good seat for you," but say to the poor man, "You stand there" or "Sit on the floor by my feet," have you not discriminated among yourselves and become judges with evil thoughts?

JAMES 2:3-4

Lord,

I thank You that You do not show favoritism or prejudice toward the people You have created. Thank You that any human being can be clothed with Christ no matter what his or her religious background, social status, gender, race, or color (Gal. 3:27-28). Today I ask that You would increase my understanding that in You we are all one—and You are over all and in all (Col. 3:11).

I know that I stand guilty of having different attitudes toward people based on their clothing or beauty or race (James 2:2). It happens so subtly, Lord! Without even meaning to, I buy into the myth that a well-dressed person is somehow smarter, somehow more valuable than a person who can't afford the right labels. Please forgive me. Help me not to hold unfair opinions or reactions based on such things as money, clothes, or position (1 Tim. 5:21).

Father, please help me to make my home a place where we do what is right by loving our neighbor as ourselves—and without partiality (James 2:8). May we be a shining example of a willingness to go against the crowd, not only accepting those who are different, but embracing them.

Amen.

Be Here!

*What other nation is so great as to have their gods near them
the way the LORD our God is near us whenever we pray to him?*

DEUTERONOMY 4:7

Father,

You are near to everyone who calls out Your name (Ps. 34:15). You
draw close to everyone who tries to draw close to You (James 4:8).

I call. I draw close. I revel in Your presence right now!

*I live in a high and holy place, but also with him who is contrite and
lowly in spirit* (Isa. 57:15).

Thank You, Lord. Show me anything in my heart or life that
grieves You. Your gracious presence is all I need.

For myself, my family, and those who walk with me in the faith
today, I ask: Unstuff our ears, open our eyes, melt our hearts with Your
compelling reality. Your ability to be near us every moment is guaranteed, but our ability to see and hear You is shaky at best. But we belong
to You, and You love the fellowship of Your people (Ps. 14:5).

Be here! Be here! In ringing phones and silent hallways, crowded
highways and lonely decisions, stressful meetings and lazy conversations,
silly mistakes and smashing successes—in every moment of our day, be
here among us, O God!

I am always with you. It is good to be near Me (from Ps. 73:23,28).

Yes, You are here. And it is good to be near You. Let Your Spirit
sing in my innermost being today. And may I sing in You and bring
You joy.

Amen.

Please Help Me Change

Take away the disgrace I dread.... Preserve my life in your righteousness.

Lord,

Please help me change. Sometimes I treat others in ways that seem to spring from negative past experiences. Almost helplessly, I watch myself repeating relationship habits that have never worked—but I seem to do them anyway.

Show me a new way, Lord. I know that wounds from sins can be passed down from generation to generation (Exod. 34:6-7). I also know that bondages can be broken as I face and forgive the past. Today please begin to break any of those chains that remain, and bring me the healing I need, Lord (Isa. 42:7).

"Heal me, O LORD, and I will be healed; save me and I will be saved" (Jer. 17:14).

Surround me with friends who will heal me with kind truths (Prov. 27:6), and help me to listen carefully to them. Reveal to me the areas where I need to forgive, or to make different, healthier choices for myself and my family. You are able to use for good even those years in my past that were sometimes painful (Joel 2:25).

But I will restore you to health and heal your wounds. Forget the former things; do not dwell on the past. See, I am doing a new thing! (Jer. 30:17; Isa. 43:18-19).

Yes, Lord, do a new thing in my life today. Help me to know what to accept as part of my God-given humanity, and what I should watch closely for new shoots of change.

Amen.

To Pray Is to Change

o pray is to change. Prayer is the central avenue God uses to transform us. If we are unwilling to change, we will abandon prayer as a noticeable characteristic in our lives. The closer we come to the heartbeat of God the more we see our need and the more we desire to be conformed to Christ....

In prayer, real prayer, we begin to think God's thoughts after Him, to desire the things He desires, to love the things He loves. Progressively we are taught to see things from His point of view.

RICHARD FOSTER

Abraham's Gift

Abraham built an altar there and arranged the wood on it. He bound
his son Isaac and laid him on the altar, on top of the wood. Then he
reached out his hand and took the knife to slay his son. But the angel of
the LORD called out to him from heaven, "Abraham! Abraham!" "Here I
am," he replied. "Do not lay a hand on the boy," he said. "Do not do
anything to him. Now I know that you fear God, because you have not
withheld from me your son, your only son." Abraham looked up and
there in a thicket he saw a ram caught by its horns. He went over and
took the ram and sacrificed it as a burnt offering instead of his son. So
Abraham called that place The LORD Will Provide.

GENESIS 22:9-14

Heavenly Father,

What was going through Abraham's mind while he was tying up his
only child? What did he say to the frightened, confused boy? How did
he explain the "God of Abraham" to his son then?

You asked Abraham for everything: his happiness, his future, even
the very gift (Isaac, "child of promise") that You'd given him and Sarah
in their old age. But Abraham believed in who You were, even when
what You were doing seemed disastrous, awful, unexplainable.

You needed that kind of faith from him—resolute but pure, radical
but childlike, "afraid" of God but at peace with Him—to accomplish
Your beautiful plan. You wanted someone to demonstrate how far You'd
go with Your only Son, Jesus, to show Your Father-love for us.

Father, I humbly pray for Abraham's gift of faith today.

In Jesus' name. Amen.

Five Steps

*Be on your guard; stand firm in the faith; be men of courage; be strong.
Do everything in love.*

1 CORINTHIANS 16:13-14

Lord,

Today I pray according to Paul's instruction to new believers who felt
pulled in every direction by the culture around them. I want to be true
to You, and to express Your true-ness all day long.

Be on your guard—Show me, Lord, the influences, distractions, or
downright attacks that could pierce my spirit or get me off track from
this spiritual adventure with You.

Stand firm in the faith—Help me remember today the unchange-
able truths I'm building my life on: God is real; God is love; God is life;
God has requirements; I can't reach or please God on my own, but in
Christ, God has made a way back to Himself.

Be people of courage—You've made me with feelings that fly one
way, then another, then hang limp like the flag at the courthouse. Show
me when to trust, and when to distrust, my feelings today. Help me to
act brave even when I don't feel it.

Be strong—Help me reach for Your promised strength today. Keep
me from compromises that weaken my commitment and sabotage my
success. Put Your shield of spiritual safety around me.

Do everything in love—Yes, everything. But how? Only by Your
presence, which is Love, reaching beyond the stingy limits of my own
inclinations today. Oh, especially help me to love, Lord!

In Your name I pray. Amen.

Bigmouth

When words are many, sin is not absent, but he who holds his tongue is wise.

PROVERBS 10:19

Lord Jesus,

How many words are many? Chances are, dear Lord, I speak too many. Today my prayer is that You would help me to embark on a serious "word diet." Show me how to speak fewer words and more wisdom:

With words of affirmation—not quick words of criticism—let me encourage and uplift those I know best (Prov. 12:14).

With words of discretion and patience—not reckless words that pierce like a sword—let me be a wise friend who brings healing (Prov. 12:18).

With words of compassion—not careless gossip or slander—bless my conversations with those I work or play with today (Ps. 34:12-14).

With soft words of kindness—not sarcastic or cutting remarks—help me wash away all bitterness, anger, or upset between me and those I love (Eph. 4:31-32; Prov. 15:1).

With words of respect—not defensiveness or self-righteousness—may every conversation I have today be gentle, courteous, and full of mercy (Titus 3:2; James 3:17, TLB).

Thank You, Lord, that You are a meek and gentle Savior who can change even bigmouths like me.

Amen.

Scaredy-Cat

For I am the LORD, your God, who takes hold of your right hand and says to you, Do not fear; I will help you.

ISAIAH 41:13

Heavenly Father,

How kind of You to care about the scaredy-cat I live with almost every day! Fear of harm, anxieties about the unknown, recurring insecurities, nameless dreads—these preoccupations claw away Your peace. They yowl in my thoughts till I can't hear You. They keep me cornered.

Teach me today about the Father God who always holds my hand, who is ready to reassure me, "Don't be afraid; I will help you."

I will never leave you helpless. I'll never let you down. I'll never let go of you! (from Heb. 13:5).

Does my fear start when I measure my resources against my needs (real or imagined) and come up short? The best fix for my fear then is grasping Your personal, unshakable commitment to my well-being. You've given me Your own Spirit of power, love, and self-discipline (2 Tim. 1:7). I can live free, confident that I'm Yours. Day or night, I can call, "Abba, Father!" and You'll hear and care (Rom. 8:15).

Take courage! It is I. Don't be afraid (Mark 6:50).

You've said that a prudent person sees real danger and takes refuge; the fool keeps charging ahead (Prov. 22:3). Teach me to fear wisely. Is my feeling a God-given warning sign to be heeded, or is it faithless, self-preoccupied fretting?

Bring this encouragement to mind today: *The Lord is my helper; I will not be afraid* (Heb. 13:6).

Amen.

Full of Confidence

In quietness and confidence is your strength.

ISAIAH 30:15, NLT

MEDITATIONS FOR YOUR DAY

I'm confident of this,
that God who began a good work in _____
will carry it on to completion until the
day Jesus returns.
(from Phil. 1:6)

I am confident through Christ—
not that I can claim any special powers for myself,
but my competence comes from God.
By His Spirit, He has made me competent
as a minister of new life in Christ.
(from 2 Cor. 3:4-6)

Now this I can count on:
Even if _____ is faithless,
God will remain faithful!
(from 2 Tim. 2:11,13)

For Better or Worse

So the LORD God banished him from the Garden of Eden to work the ground from which he had been taken.

Heavenly Father,

How quickly the easy bliss of those first lovers in Eden turned into bitter trials. Love that had been innocent, safe, and effortless suddenly required commitment, forgiveness, and hard work.

As far as we know, You didn't ask Adam and Eve to exchange marriage vows (Gen. 2:22-25). But theirs was the ultimate example of enduring both good times and bad. They shared love first in a perfect Eden and afterward in a difficult exile (Gen. 3:23).

Hear our own "after Eden" marriage prayer today: We want to be faithful to the vows we made—to love each other "for better or for worse, for richer or for poorer, in sickness and in health."

We know that each of our vows will be tested by life—that marriage doesn't let us escape the consequences of our fallen world. In fact, your Word tells us, "He who finds a wife finds what is good" (Prov. 18:22), but it also says, "Those who marry will face many troubles in this life" (1 Cor. 7:28). Lord, we accept the reality of both—the better and the worse.

And Lord, how wonderful are those "better" times—when we glimpse Eden in our romance and in the passionate wonders of sexual love. Yes, we happily praise You for the times when we are healthy, getting along well, and richly blessed!

But today show us also the hidden opportunities in those painful, "worse" times—when conflicts, sickness, and financial pressures weigh heavily upon us. It is harder to feel grateful for these things. But we know You use weaknesses and trials to test and strengthen us and our marriage (James 1:2-4).

And this is truly what we desire, Lord! We want to learn to love at all times (Prov. 17:17.) We want a relationship that is full of kindness, patience, faith, and hope. We want a love that will never fail (1 Cor. 13:4-8).

Right now, we stand in Your presence to embrace once more those sacred marriage vows. Yes, Lord, today we choose each other all over again—for better or worse.

We praise and thank You, God of love before and after Eden. Amen.

Lord of All My Being

In him we live and move and have our being.

ACTS 17:28

PRAYING WITH THE SARUM PRIMER PRAYER

Great Lord,

If You pour Yourself into me until I'm full, and if I receive You completely, and if You sweep out every sin and I let go of every one, then I'll have all I need. Because my being—the most me I can be—is made for You. Be Lord of all of my being today.

> *God be in my head and in my understanding.*
> "We have the mind of Christ" (1 Cor. 2:16).
> Yes, Lord, may I understand and value everything
> with Your Spirit-born insights today.

> *God be in my eyes and in my looking.*
> "Let us fix our eyes on Jesus, the author and perfecter
> of our faith" (Heb. 12:2).
> Yes, Lord, may You be the focus of all my attentions
> and the judge of all my pursuits and passions today.

> *God be in my mouth and in my speaking.*
> "Let the word of Christ dwell in you richly as you teach and admonish
> one another with all wisdom" (Col. 3:16).
> Yes, Lord, may I speak with Your wisdom, Your gentleness,
> and Your life-giving goodness today.

God be in my heart and in my thinking.
"Your attitude should be the same as that of Christ Jesus" (Phil. 2:5).
Yes, Lord, may my desires and attitudes reveal
and extend to everyone around me
Your beautiful nature today.

God be at my end and at my departing.
"For to me, to live is Christ and to die is gain" (Phil. 1:21).
Yes, Lord, may I cherish each day as a gift from You to be lived for You
and receive with assurance Your promise of eternity
to be lived with You.
Amen.

Standing on the Promises

He has given us his very great and precious promises.

2 PETER 1:4

Dear Heavenly Father,

I grew up singing the hymn "Standing on the Promises," but mostly I was standing because I had to, waiting for church to get out. Now as an adult, I understand the song. Without Your promises, Christians have no hope. If You don't keep Your Word, we're sunk.

But thank You that You are a God of Your word (Num. 23:19). Like string around a priceless package, Your pledge of kindness holds all our hopes together (Neh. 9:17-25). How I thank You today for the promises in the Bible.

I claim these "great and precious promises" right now—think about them, plant them in my memory, resolve to act confidently upon them all through my day.

—"Never will I leave you; never will I forsake you" (Heb. 13:5).

—"I am your provider and protector, comforter and friend" (from Ps. 23:1; 27:1; Isa. 25:8; John 15:15).

—"If two of you on earth agree about anything you ask for, it will be done for you" (Matt. 18:19).

—"Everyone who receives me and believes in my name becomes a child of God" (from John 1:12).

—"My kindness, mercies, and love for you are inexhaustible" (from Ps. 18:50; Ps. 25:6; Jer. 31:3).

Claim means, "They're mine!" But I also claim them for other spiritual pilgrims I could encourage today. And for lost searchers I meet who doubt that You exist or that You are good.

I praise You and exalt You today that "every word of God is flawless" (Prov. 30:5) and that "forever, O LORD, thy word is settled in heaven" (Ps. 119:89, KJV).

Because God wanted to make the unchanging nature of his purpose very clear to the heirs of what was promised, he confirmed it with an oath. God did this so that, by two unchangeable things in which it is impossible for God to lie, we who have fled to take hold of the hope offered to us may be greatly encouraged. We have this hope as an anchor for the soul, firm and secure (Heb. 6:17-19).

Thank You, Father.

Amen.

Sweeter Than Honey

How sweet are your words to my taste.

PSALM 119:103

PRAYING FROM PSALM 19

Heavenly Father,

Today I meditate on the sweetness and appeal of the Bible—wonderful words of life!

Your laws are perfect, reviving the soul (v. 7). Bring new life where there is only decay or sluggishness. How much I need Your refreshment. How sweet is Your Word to my taste!

Your statutes are trustworthy (v. 7). If I'm counting on them to be true and reliable, I can lean far out, I can build up high, I can reach for great things. Help me trust each biblical teaching and principle today. How sweet is Your Word to my taste!

Your precepts are right, giving joy to the heart (v. 8). Yes, living Your way makes happy people! May I and those around me take gen-uine delight in studying the Bible so we understand Your joy makers. How sweet is Your Word to my taste!

Your commands are radiant, giving light to the eyes (v. 8). Lead me to Yourself in Your words, and to the wisdom You've promised. When I need direction, understanding and encouragement, open my spiritual eyes to Your truths. How sweet is Your Word to my taste!

To live in reverent fear of the Lord is pure, enduring forever (v. 9). Help me get ready for the beautiful soundtrack of eternity—angels and redeemed sinners worshiping You. Please be teaching me how to revere and honor You all day long. How sweet is Your Word to my taste!

Your guidelines are sure and altogether fair (v. 9, NLT). Help me to rely on the Bible to test every other belief, philosophy, or lifestyle I encounter. How sweet is Your Word to my taste!

Yes, Your Word is truly sweeter than honey (v. 10). I want to crave time in the Bible more than any other reading or viewing matter today. Thank You, Lord, that You've promised great personal reward as a result (v. 11). How sweet is Your Word to my taste!

I exclaim with Jeremiah today: "When your words came, I ate them; they were my joy and my heart's delight, for I bear your name, O LORD God Almighty" (Jer. 15:16).

Yes, how sweet is Your Word to my taste!

Amen.

The Word Makes a Way

It is not mere words that nourish the soul, but God himself.... The Bible is not an end in itself, but a means to bring men to an intimate and satisfying knowledge of God, that they may enter into Him, that they may delight in His Presence, may taste and know the inner sweetness of the very God Himself in the core and center of their hearts.

A. W. TOZER

Master of the House

I will walk in my house with a blameless heart. I will set before my eyes no vile thing.

PSALM 101:2-3

Heavenly Lord,

You stand at the door of my house and knock. I hear Your voice and open the door. Please come in. Please take up residence and build a relationship here (Rev. 3:20). This place is set apart for You—You are Lord here (1 Pet. 3:15)!

Today I rededicate my home and my life to You. With Joshua I say, "As for me and my household, we will serve the LORD" (Josh. 24:15). Help us to keep out any object or activity that would offend You, Master of the house. We want to be blameless before You (Ps. 101:2-3).

May the power and healing of Your Word be the mark of this home, posted on doors, gates, and refrigerators (Deut. 6:9). May unity and harmony be the glue that holds us together (Mark 3:24). May biblical wisdom put into practice create gracious and sensible lifestyles here, as apparent to everyone as seven carved pillars out front (Prov. 9:1).

May a ready hospitality to both friends and strangers be our goal (Rom. 12:13; Heb. 13:2; 1 Pet. 4:9). May every visitor recognize right away that You are in this place—exclaiming inwardly, "How awesome is this place! This is none other than the house of God" (Gen. 28:16-17).

And may our worship of You in every conversation and activity fill each room like the fragrance of expensive perfume (John 12:3).

Yes, You're Master of these rooms. Unless You are Master, every effort is wasted (Ps. 127:1). Come in again today. Please come in.

Amen.

The Fool Factor

He who walks with the wise grows wise, but a companion of fools suffers harm.

PROVERBS 13:20

PRAYING FROM PROVERBS

Lord,

Your Word is so full of "do not's" about the wrong crowd: "Do not envy wicked men, do not desire their company..." (24:1); "Do not join those who drink too much wine..." (23:20); "If sinners entice you, do not give in to them..." (1:10). Teach me how to steer clear of the wrong friends.

Show me how to be a fair judge of character without unfairly judging a person's worth. And show me how to know the difference between friends I can lean on and needy people who may need to lean on me for a while. I don't want to live selfishly, just wisely.

Yes, how much I need Your wisdom, Lord. The world often seems to favor the "do not" crowd. Music and the media make heroes out of all kinds of lazy, dishonest, and dangerous people (1:10-19). But they're all headed for trouble eventually—and I'll catch it too if I just go with the flow.

Open my eyes to the truth. Intervene with Your grace and protection when necessary, especially when those who are driven by evil desires try to lure me into danger. Help me to recognize the wrong crowd for who they are—rebels who struggle along without Your blessing (3:33).

Amen.

The Healing Touch

When Jesus came into Peter's house, he saw Peter's mother-in-law lying in bed with a fever. He touched her hand and the fever left her, and she got up and began to wait on him. When evening came, many who were demon-possessed were brought to him, and he drove out the spirits with a word and healed all the sick. This was to fulfill what was spoken through the prophet Isaiah: "He took up our infirmities and carried our diseases."

MATTHEW 8:14-17

Dear Lord,

Because You cared about a mother-in-law with fever, and touched her hand, and healed her; because Peter didn't have to ask; because You cared too for the poor, twisted souls ravaged by Satan, and spoke a word, and healed them back to wholeness and dignity where they had known only shame and shunning…

I can trust You with my requests for healing today. In my family, these are my concerns: _____ and _____. For the ill in my community (some of whom I'd probably rather avoid), these are my requests: _____ and _____ and _____. With the centurion, I confess, "Lord I do not deserve to have you come under my roof. But just say the word, and _____ will be healed" (Matt. 8:8).

Thank You, compassionate Lord, that You care about the flu and cold sweats and in-laws. Thank You that You reach out to the hopeless with a word of hope. Thank You that You are stronger than Satan.

I will restore you to health and heal your wounds (Jer. 30:17).

I praise You for hearing my prayer, Lord Jesus.

Amen.

The Grace of Giving

But just as you excel in everything—in faith, in speech, in knowledge, in complete earnestness and in your love for us—see that you also excel in this grace of giving.

2 CORINTHIANS 8:7

Heavenly Father,

I confess, I'm just a beginner at giving. Sometimes it hurts to give, like trying to lift a piano—as if, just maybe, I was born to get instead.

But You say it is better to give than to receive (Acts 20:35). You say give to those who take (Matt 5:40-42). You say give freely, as it has been given to me (Matt. 10:8). You say give, and it will be given back (Luke 6:38).

Lord, is there a gift—of time, attention, encouragement, a word, a smile, labor, money—that would "be Christ" to another today (Mark 9:41)? Is there a major task or commitment You've been trying to turn my attention to (Luke 9:23)? I'm ready to discover, like the early Christians, that hiding somewhere in my troubles and even "extreme poverty" there is a "rich generosity" waiting to be shared (2 Cor. 8:2).

Anoint me with the grace of giving today, Father—to give cheerfully, diligently, freely, and purely (2 Cor. 9:7). How You excel at giving, Father! Every good thing in my life is from You (James 1:17). Your generosity is my wealth (Prov. 10:22). You paid the ultimate price to give me life and a future (John 3:16).

Thank You that I've been born again—this time, to give.
Amen.

I'm No Angel

For we know that our old self was crucified with him so that the body of sin might be done away with, that we should no longer be slaves to sin—because anyone who has died has been freed from sin.

ROMANS 6:6-7

PRAYING FROM ROMANS 6–8

Lord,

If you made me free from sin, why does it stick to me like manure on my boots? If my old self is dead—nailed on the cross with Your body—why does it haunt and bully me so?

By Your Spirit, show me a better way. Lead me in Your Truth. I want to honor You, my God, with my life and with my choices—even those hidden choices of attitude and priority and motive that no one sees but You. How I long to be clean forever of the manure of sin and rebellion!

I exclaim with Paul: "I do not understand what I do. For what I want to do I do not do, but what I hate I do.... I have the desire to do what is good, but I cannot carry it out" (7:15,18).

Thank You that even though I'm still a fallen human, I don't have to live under Your condemnation for my shortcomings. The "sin offering" of Jesus covers me fully (8:1-4). Thank You that in some real, ongoing way that I don't understand, Your Spirit's power is always at work in those who "have their minds set on what the Spirit desires" (8:5).

Yes, help me to set my mind on what You desire today:

—to remember the genuine contentment and reward that pleasing You brings (8:6),

—to make You resident monitor of all my thoughts and attitudes (8:9),

—to give complete ownership of my life to You because I belong to You; to give the Spirit occupancy rights in my heart (8:9),

—to "put to death"—don't coddle, excuse, compromise with, associate with, or in any way nurture—the impulses and behaviors I know are wrong (8:13),

—to listen to Your Spirit's leading in all my decisions and activities—and quickly obey (8:14),

—to breathe Your name—"Abba, Father"—all day long, keeping a thankful heart for the eternal inheritance that being in Your family provides (8:15-17).

By Your Spirit living in me, give new life to this commitment today. Even raise it from the dead, like You did Jesus, if you have to (8:11)!

Thank You that You do not judge me according to the record of my performance but by the merits of Your grace (6:14). I'll never be an angel, but I don't have to be a sin-slave either.

Amen.

Heart of a Disciple

The heart is deceitful above all things and beyond cure. Who can understand it? I the LORD search the heart.

JEREMIAH 17:9-10

O Lord— my Lord,
Yes, I call You Lord. You are the Christ, the One to make my life complete. Like Peter, I leap to name You my King (Matt. 16:16); I set You apart in my heart as first (1 Peter 3:15). But I still want to be first too (Mark 8:33-35). Like Andrew, I love to talk to my friends and family about You (John 1:41), but sometimes—especially under stress—I pretend, like Peter, that I don't know You (Luke 22:57). Like John, I love to be loved by You, to be Your special child (John 13:23), but when Your teachings get inconvenient or hard, I'm quick to look for an easier gospel (John 6:66). Just when taking a stand is needed, I tend to turn and run (Matt. 26:56).
When I have doubts, too often, as with Thomas, You have to come looking for me (John 20:24-28). And if You don't deliver what I think a "God" should, I'm guilty, like Judas, of betraying You, Your amazing record of goodness, and Your authority in my life (John 18:2-3). Forgive me! Lord, in my inner being, I delight in Your law (Rom. 7:22), but I don't understand—what I want to do I do not do, but what I hate I do (Rom. 7:15). You know the secrets of my heart, Lord (Ps. 44:21).
Create in me a heart that's new and whole and Yours all through (Ezek. 18:31).
Amen.

Joy Returns

When Jehovah brought back his exiles to Jerusalem, it was like a dream!
How we laughed and sang for joy. And the other nations said, "What
amazing things the Lord has done for them." Yes, glorious things! What
wonder! What joy! May we be refreshed as by streams in the desert. Those
who sow tears shall reap joy. Yes, they go out weeping, carrying seed for
sowing, and return singing, carrying their sheaves.

PSALM 126, TLB

Lord God,
I just want to thank You this morning—You, so high above my life—
for the joy that returns. You stoop down to anoint my spirit with comfort and peace.

Thank You for Your invading goodness, the kindnesses that You
leave just inside the door of my days. Thank You for the relentless mercies that pursue me when I stray. Thank You for carrying my sorrows
like a tender Father.

You saw in the seeds of tears the harvest fields to come. You heard
in yesterday's grief today's music. Thank You for the joy that returns.

I don't need happiness today, or highs, or thrills. I don't need cli-
maxes or excitement or breakthroughs or success. I float in Your joy—
the balm of Jesus—these waters of contentment on which I drift like a
yellow boat in the morning on a still, still pond.

What amazing things You've done for me!

What wonder!

What joy!

Amen.

Longing for Home

All these people were still living by faith when they died. They did not receive the things promised; they only saw them and welcomed them from a distance. And they admitted that they were aliens and strangers on earth.... They were longing for a better country—a heavenly one. Therefore God is not ashamed to be called their God, for he has prepared a city for them.

HEBREWS 11:13,16

Heavenly Father,
Something in me wants to settle in today...
    to belong...
    to put down roots like a massive oak...
    to be part of the land—immovable and enduring.

Change wears me out. Yet rapid, continual, and mostly unwanted change seems to describe my life. I long to belong, to be secure and stationary. But life hurtles along, restless and shifting. And when life slows, You're often the one to step out in front and lead me forward...
    Again.

You are not of this world. You have set your heart on pilgrimage. You will be blessed as you find your strength in me (from John 17:16; Ps. 84:5).

Yes, Lord, today I feel all out of place. Dropped off on the wrong roadside—and no one's stopping to pick me up. Your strength feels far away. Peter's words howl in my thoughts like truck tires rolling past: "strangers"..."scattered"..."alien"... (1 Pet. 1:1-2; 2:11).

Did you really mean for us to live in tents? For motion to be the constant and only the intervals to be spent in one place?

Teach me today from Your Word and Your Spirit. I want to learn from Abraham—wanderer, fugitive, man of faith (Heb. 11:8-10). You called him friend (Isa. 41:8). You were proud to be his God.

Help me pull up stakes today, pick up my bag. You will be the theme of my song wherever I camp (Ps. 119:54). I'll trust You to take me from strength to strength until I finally reach home—eternity in Your presence (Ps. 84:7).

In the name of Jesus, who had nowhere to lay His head (Luke 9:58). Amen.

Love Like Yours

But go and learn what this means: "I desire mercy, not sacrifice." For I have not come to call the righteous, but sinners.

MATTHEW 9:13

Jesus, friend of sinners,
I'm so grateful for Your questing love! I was a castaway who desperately needed rescuing, and You saved me! Teach me today to care about the ones You cared about so passionately—those with social, physical, or personality "liabilities." Let me share Your radical, healing "social grace."

It's so easy for me to reject or judge unbelievers who pursue an openly immoral lifestyle. But You defended an adulterous woman who was dragged before You to be judged: "If any one of you is without sin, let him be the first to throw a stone" (John 8:7).

Deliver me from my arrogant tendency to shun people I think of as losers. What a shamefully long list I could make, Lord. Yet I remember Your words to the prostitute who "wasted" perfume on Your feet: "Her many sins have been forgiven—for she loved much" (Luke 7:47).

Help me change my lazy and selfish habit of socializing only with those who already know You. You told a disbelieving seeker: "God did not send his Son into the world to condemn the world, but to save the world through him" (John 3:17).

When I meet one person today of the sort You came down from heaven to look for—a sinner worth dying for—help me to have love like Yours. I want to express the same quality of kindness and caring that You have so often granted me (Luke 23:34): "For the Son of Man came to seek and to save what was lost" (Luke 19:10).

Amen.

Comfort for the Journey

Do not let your hearts be troubled. Trust in God; trust also in me. In my Father's house are many rooms; if it were not so, I would have told you. I am going there to prepare a place for you. And if I go and prepare a place for you, I will come back and take you to be with me that you also may be where I am.

JOHN 14:1-3

MEDITATIONS FOR YOUR DAY

Since you are receiving a kingdom that cannot be shaken,
be thankful, and so worship God acceptably with reverence and awe.
(from Heb. 12:28)

Blessed are those whose strength is in you,
who have set their hearts on pilgrimage.
As they pass through the Valley of Baca,
they make it a place of springs;
the autumn rains also cover it with pools.
They go from strength to strength,
till each appears before God in Zion.
(Ps. 84:5-7)

False Confidence

When pride comes, then comes disgrace, but with humility comes wisdom.

PROVERBS 11:2

Heavenly Father,

Pride comes so easily to me, I confess. And when it arrives, it feels like confidence, self-esteem, or strength. Maybe pride is so easy because it's a flattering lie. But Your Word tells me it soon leads to a fall (Prov. 16:18), and I agree. How dangerous and weak the wrong kind of confidence can be!

Help me to understand that a humble spirit will be blessed and guided by You (Ps. 25:9). Be teaching me today the difference between thinking too much of myself and seeing myself accurately (Rom. 12:3). Grow me up in my spirit so that I will love the praise of God more than the praise of men (John 12:43).

You've promised that if I approach You with humility, You will lift me up (James 4:10). You will help me achieve the right kind of success with attitudes that please You and bless others. What strengths do I have that You didn't give me anyway?

May I remember the radical teaching of Jesus today: "The meek and lowly are fortunate! for the whole wide world belongs to them" (Matt. 5:5, TLB).

Amen.

Together We Stand

A city or home divided against itself cannot stand.

MATTHEW 12:25, TLB

Lord of Peace,

You say it is good and pleasant when brothers and sisters live together in harmony (Ps. 133:1). You pour out Your blessing like anointing oil when Your children get along (Ps. 133:2).

I pray for peace in the family today—my home, my extended family, my church family, the family of Your followers in the world. The first Christians were so changed by their new faith that they were one in heart and mind (Acts 4:32). And they turned the known world upside down (Acts 17:6, KJV). What power is released by believers at peace!

Prince of Peace, without your help I don't think we can live like that!

Please grant Your help today, Your very presence and anointing of unity. Show me right now by Your Spirit where dis-ease and dissension, arguing and striving are preventing You from working.

Yes, I pray especially about: _____, _____, _____. Let me be the first to lay down those ugly battle weapons—my own rights and preferences, my own memories of little injustices, old habits of nagging, teasing, or provoking another. Show me instead how to pick up the building blocks of peace—pure motives, thoughtfulness, submission, fairness, mercy, and love (James 3:17). And I pray this for those You mention in my spirit now as well.

Breathe upon us Your powerful Spirit of unity today, so that with one, clear voice Your family on earth may glorify You (Rom. 15:5) and show to the world that You are real (John 17:23).

Amen.

Money Matters

The rich rule over the poor, and the borrower is servant to the lender.

Heavenly Father,

Teach me Your wisdom about money. Money is both a power and a curse (Prov. 13:8), an illusion and a reality (Luke 8:14). Money opens up new vistas of opportunity but can leave me blind in the process (Ps. 39:6; Mark 10:23). It makes everything run better (Eccles. 7:12; 10:19) but keeps me running in hot pursuit long after I want to quit (Eccles. 5:10-11).

Most of all, money is a reflection of my true allegiances. Lord, may how I think about and use money in my life reveal priorities that honor You. All my life, bring the role money plays under Your full authority.

May money never be my master; that is Your position alone, sovereign Lord (Matt. 6:24). Forgive me when I wear myself out to get ahead when it could all be gone tomorrow (Prov. 23:4).

May making money or scrambling for the pleasures, position, or security that wealth promises never be my passion in life. That kind of misdirected zeal only brings sorrows and troubles of many kinds (1 Tim. 6:10). You are the One I seek after with my whole heart; Your blessing is my greatest wealth, and no blight comes with what You give (Ps. 119:58; Prov. 10:22, TLB).

May money never define my role in the community; may good works, love, and a reputation for earnestly seeking Your path do that (Rom. 12:9-17). I pray for enough financial security to be free of want, but not so much that it corrupts Your purposes in my life (Prov. 30:8-9).

May careless or irresponsible spending never leave me in want, or even worse, in debt. That kind of lazy disregard for prudent money management is a sin against Your kindness (James 1:17). Forgive me, Father.

Help me to learn this ancient wisdom for handling my assets:

—valuing simplicity with integrity (Prov. 14:30; 15:16-17)

—respecting the honor of honest work (Prov. 12:11; 14:23)

—taking care of what I have (Prov. 12:27)

—saving for future needs (Prov. 13:11)

—investing for capital growth (Prov. 31:14-18)

—giving generously to those in need, especially those in the community of faith (Prov. 11:24-25)

—tithing a regular percentage to my church and to Your work and Your servants around the world (Prov. 3:9-10)

I know that every good thing is from You, Father (James 1:17). May how I handle money be just another expression of my daily gratitude to You. Yes, may every dollar saved or spent identify me with Your eternal purposes in my life. Please help me, because money makes such a fool (and a traitor) out of me.

Amen.

Holy Confidence

We will shout for joy when you are victorious and will lift up our banners in the name of our God.

PSALM 20:5

A BLESSING FROM PSALM 20:1-4

May the Lord answer you today
when you're in distress.
May God's power protect you,
and may His names—"Refuge," "Provider," "Almighty"—
infuse you with holy confidence.
May His angel warriors guard you,
and may the prayers of His people surround you.
May He grant your heart's desire
And make all your plans succeed.

Bread of Life

Now there was a man of the Pharisees named Nicodemus, a member of the Jewish ruling council. He came to Jesus at night and said, "Rabbi, we know you are a teacher who has come from God. For no one could perform the miraculous signs you are doing if God were not with him." In reply Jesus declared, "I tell you the truth, no one can see the kingdom of God unless he is born again." "How can a man be born when he is old?" Nicodemus asked.

JOHN 3:1-4

Dear Lord Jesus,

Because You argued with lawyers and experts, with seekers and doubters; because You stayed up late into the night to answer dumb questions from one seeking soul who couldn't quite grasp what "born again" could possibly mean, but wanted to…

I pray today for the ones I know You're seeking, those who need so desperately to be found. I'm thinking especially of _____, _____, and _____. Thank You for placing these seekers in my life. Reveal Yourself and Your truth to them through my willingness to speak and live for You today. I pray with Paul "that whenever I open my mouth, words may be given me so that I will fearlessly make known the mystery of the gospel" (Eph. 6:19).

I assure you, anyone who believes in me already has eternal life. Yes, I am the bread of life! (John 6:47-48, NLT).

Yes, complete Your redemption miracle today, O Lord of Life! Amen.

Bone Valley

*He brought me out by the Spirit of the LORD and set me in the middle
of a valley; it was full of bones. He led me back and forth among them,
and I saw a great many bones on the floor of the valley, bones that were
very dry. He asked me, "Son of man, can these bones live?" I said, "O
Sovereign LORD, you alone know."*

EZEKIEL 37:1-3

PRAYING FROM EZEKIEL 37

Sovereign Lord,

Today I'm surrounded by the bones of failure and defeat. Just bones,
the bleached-out evidence of what used to be, everywhere I look.

Can these bones live again? You know, my God.

How I wish that I'd never ended up here. How I wish that You
would have intervened to keep me from this place; interrupted my foolishness, my mistakes, my stubborn sinning; stepped in to protect me
from the cruelty of others; spared me from the tragedy in life.

Stay with me in the valley of bones, Sovereign Lord. Yes, You are
sovereign, ruling without limit, even in such lonely, human places. Jesus
willingly went to a place like this, to Golgotha, "the place of the skull."
He died there so I could live again here (Rom. 5:8; 6:23).

In this time of sorrow, breathe on me, Lord. Breathe on my life—
into a dream, a relationship, a vocation or calling, a project, a wayward
child, a deep loss… You know what's lying broken at my feet.

*I will put breath in you, and you will come to life. Then you will know
that I am the LORD* (Ezek. 37:6).

Oh, Your breath of life is enough, Lord. Like it was that first day in Eden (Gen. 2:7), like it was for Israel in Ezekiel's day. Yes, You can bring me back from any captivity or loss (Ezek. 37:12-14).

I will put my Spirit in you and you will live,...then you will know that I the LORD have...done it (v. 14).

I hear Your voice in this valley. Be glorified in these bones. Yes, turn their dry desolation into a faith-building, God-honoring triumph! Form me again with the flesh of strength, the pulse of purpose, the blood of passion, and the face of joy.

And I'll stand up and walk out of this place, Sovereign Lord.

Amen.

Nothing Is Impossible

When God is about to do some thing great,

He starts with a difficulty.

When He is about to do something truly magnificent,

He starts with an impossibility.

ARMIN GESSWEIN

Secret Hope

And this is the secret: that Christ in your hearts is your only hope of glory.

COLOSSIANS 1:27, TLB

PRAYING FROM COLOSSIANS

Dear God,

Apart from Christ's presence and power, I'm such an ordinary person. But You have made me new by Your life-giving Son (2:13). When You look at me, You see the shining beauty of Christ (3:3). What a miracle!

May that beauty continue its work in my life today:

Christ in my words; Christ in my wants.

Christ in my friendships; Christ in my loneliness.

Christ in my going and coming; Christ in my seeing and doing.

Christ in my thinking and in my praying;

Christ in my feelings and in my fingertips.

May the triumph of Christ on the cross, and the power that is mine as a result, set me free from sin (2:13-15).

May the hope and peace of Christ's nature infuse my being and surround me like a divine hug all day long (3:15).

May the words of Christ change my outlook on life and determine all my decisions, leading me in the way of wisdom (3:16).

May the joy of Christ Himself fill me with music, so that every word, thought, and action is an act of worship (3:16-17).

And for each person You bring to mind right now, this is my prayer: Christ in _____! Christ in _____! Christ in _____! And always, Christ in me!

Amen.

The Light Source

You were once darkness, but now you are light in the Lord. Live as children of light.

EPHESIANS 5:8

Father,

One of Your first recorded acts was to call the light "day" (Gen. 1:5). You are "the Father of the heavenly lights" (James 1:17), the great morning star (Isa. 14:12), and the One who turns darkness into dawn (Amos 5:8).

How thankful I am that You will never quit Your "day" job! Yet, you have also called Your children "the light of the world" (Matt. 5:14). And You have asked us to shine forth your love into the lives of those lost in shadows, blinded and confused (Eph. 4:17-19).

Help me, Father, to be faithful as a light source for You. May I never try to hide the glow within me that comes from You (Matt. 5:16). With Paul, I want to be "light in the Lord," "making the most of every opportunity" (Eph. 5:16). Shine through me into those murky deceptions around me today that pass for "culture" or "being hip." Fill my life with the fruit of the light—goodness and truth (Eph. 5:9).

Shine on, beautiful Lord of light!

In Jesus' name I pray. Amen.

Towel and Basin

It was just before the Passover Feast. Jesus knew that the time had come for him to leave this world and go to the Father. Having loved his own who were in the world, he now showed them the full extent of his love.... He got up from the meal, took off his outer clothing, and wrapped a towel around his waist. After that, he poured water into a basin and began to wash his disciples' feet, drying them with the towel that was wrapped around him.

JOHN 13:1,4-5

Dear Lord Jesus,

Because You scrubbed those dirty feet—of ordinary men who had so far demonstrated more arrogance than competence, more fickleness than faith, men who didn't even want You to be a servant but Commander-in-Chief; because You humbled Yourself in private before the ones You loved, and got on Your knees in Your briefs, and poured and scrubbed and rinsed and gently dried the feet of ordinary friends (and one of them was Judas)...

I ask today for a servant's heart. The friends and family You've placed in my life are splendid sometimes, ordinary often, and every now and then just so many dirty feet. But You undressed and got on Your knees to show them the full extent of Your love.

Show me my servant's duties today; don't let me miss them! Help me pick up towel and basin when You ask, even if no one else does.

If anyone wants to be first, he must be the very last, and the servant of all (Mark 9:35).

I make this hard request in Your name, humble Savior.

Amen.

Fish Face

From inside the fish Jonah prayed to the LORD his God. He said: "In my distress I called to the LORD, and he answered me. From the depths of the grave I called for help, and you listened to my cry."

JONAH 2:1-2

Lord God,

When I run from Your presence and Your will, You run after—
Like a wind across water, like a storm that won't stop, You pursue.
You set traps for me with truth—"I belong to God alone"—and sink
With me as I fall deep into the belly of my own small, sad rebellion.

(Jonah 1)

When I cry out in terror from some dark, stinking place, You listen,
Patient Confessor. You cherish my half-digested vows as if I'd trilled
Them from a bed of roses. "Salvation comes from the Lord!" I shout,
And, "God's grace turns every other prize to seaweed."

(Jonah 2)

When I obey and go, You travel with me to the end. In my every stutter,
Your living words surge through—and me, all acid-etched and peeled.
Your compassion rises, over and again, like the tide. Your healing oil
Shines on every lifted head. Your hope arrives like bread for beggars.

(Jonah 3)

When I'm still stung by Your extravagance, Your incautious mercies,
Your wasteful care for pimps, muggers, and whores; for cheaters and
Strangers; for enemies and pagans, for their wives and kids and cows—
You hear out my cast-up prayers, then say, "Fish Face, I'm so glad
    you're mine!"

(Jonah 4)

Word Power

Your word, O LORD, is eternal; it stands firm in the heavens.

PSALM 119:89

PRAYING FROM PSALM 119

Dear Heavenly Father,

Thank You for the Bible. What a treasure it is! I open it today in my prayers and listen again for Your voice, Your very breath on my life. So much of the rest of my day will be made up of disposable this and temporary that. How I need something firm and forever today!

Speak to me, Father. Open my eyes that I may see wonderful things in Your Word (v. 18).

When I need to know that someone cares, Your words delight me with this truth: God's compassion surrounds me (vv. 64,77)!

When I'm in the dark about things, Your Word is like a lamp to my feet and a light to my path. It shows me the best way to go (v. 105).

When I'm in danger of believing some sweet lie of temptation, Your Word keeps me from making big mistakes. Help me to store it away in my thoughts and memory like a hidden escape plan (vv. 9,11).

When my heart is worn out with sorrow, Your Word covers me like a balm, a healing, and a strength. Thank You, Lord (vv. 28,50)!

When I feel far from home or any other certainty in life, Your Word is my song and my surety. In the night, just the truth about who You are and what You've promised can banish my anxieties (vv. 54,68).

Each one of Your promises has been life-tested and proved trustworthy. That's why I savor and celebrate Your Word today (vv. 138,140).

Hear my prayer of thanks and praise. Amen.

Listening to His Words

The Bible—the revealed Word of God—is a vital part of prayer. Those with a low view of the Bible should not attempt listening prayer, for it can lead into dangerous gnostic listening. Some with a high view of Scriptures, in contrast, are prone to cordon the Bible off as though it was not a vital part of prayer. These people first study the Scriptures and then pray. But because God's basic way of revealing Himself to us is through His Son and the Holy Scriptures that bear witness to Him, we can delight in listening to God even as we read them.

LEANNE PAYNE

Pray Like This

When you pray, go into your room, close the door and pray to your Father, who is unseen. Then your Father, who sees what is done in secret, will reward you.... Your Father knows what you need before you ask him. This, then, is how you should pray.

MATTHEW 6:6,8-9

PRAYING THE LORD'S PRAYER

Heavenly Father,

Jesus taught us how to talk to You. He said, "Close the door (it's a personal relationship), pray (Your Father is listening), ask (because Your Father knows and cares)." Hear me as I pray with my Lord Jesus today:

Our Father in heaven. Yes, you are my Father, my identity, my provider and protector. My true and eventual home will be in Your presence. You are High God—"immortal, invisible"—yet I can call you "Daddy" (Rom. 8:15).

Hallowed be your name. Let me say Your names—"Father," "Lord," "Only God"—with proper awe and fear today. You are holy, so completely apart from and above me, Father. Yet I can call out Your name with confidence (Heb. 4:16). And when You turn to answer, You see me clothed in Jesus' beautiful robes of "righteousness, holiness and redemption" (1 Cor. 1:30). Thank You! Let Your name be the treasure of my talk today.

Your kingdom come, your will be done on earth as it is in heaven. (This is the hard part, Lord.) My prayers should first be about Your kingdom, Your purposes, You. Then let it be so, my God. Be King of my life today. In the big picture, show me Your every requirement and wish (Ps. 119:33-35), and help me do it. In the details—of my daydreams, cash, phone calls, free time, jokes, compliments—order my life to Your liking. Through my feeble willingness, bring a piece of heaven to earth today.

Give us today our daily bread. Yes, Lord, it's not the company, or the bank, or the national economy that gives me what I need to survive (forgive my misdirected confidences). It's You. And it's not wealth and comfort and status I have to have (forgive my insatiable greed). It's just the basics for today. In my whole life, Lord, You've never left me abandoned and starving (Ps. 37:25). You open Your hand, and I'm satisfied (Ps. 145:16). Praise You!

Forgive us our debts, as we also have forgiven our debtors. O Father, no matter how hard I try (and sometimes I don't try at all), I can't stay ahead of my debts: the ways I've injured and disappointed those I love, my convenient omissions and forgetfulness, my constant turning away from You. Forgiveness is my only hope. Teach me today to forgive those who've wronged me with the same sincerity that I ask for it now.

And lead us not into temptation, but deliver us from the evil one. Save me from "perfectly sensible" decisions, Lord. Rescue me from stupid indulgences and errors. And keep me awake to Satan's traps—they lurk everywhere just out of sight. Show me the escape routes You've promised (1 Cor. 10:13). So often, my very nature is at war with You, Father! Renew me today with the "new self" You can create in me by Your amazing power (Col. 3:10).

For yours is the kingdom and the power and the glory forever. Yes, You are Lord and King of heaven and earth. And You are my Father. For my life today, I give You all worship, all ownership, all honor.

I pray to You with Jesus' help today, in His love, by His saving grace, meditating on the words of His own prayer to You.

Amen.

Joseph's Run

The LORD was with Joseph and he prospered...in the house of his
Egyptian master.... Potiphar put him in charge of his household, and he
entrusted to his care everything he owned...with Joseph in charge, he did
not concern himself with anything except the food he ate. Now Joseph
was well-built and handsome, and after a while his master's wife took
notice of Joseph and said, "Come to bed with me!" But he refused....
"My master has withheld nothing from me except you, because you are
his wife. How then could I do such a wicked thing and sin against
God?" And though she spoke to Joseph day after day, he refused to go to
bed with her or even be with her. One day he went into the house to
attend to his duties, and none of the household servants was inside. She
caught him by his cloak and said, "Come to bed with me!" But he left
his cloak in her hand and ran out of the house.

GENESIS 39:2-12

Heavenly Father,

I love this story of a young man's unwillingness to trade away Your favor
for someone else's favor or for his own pleasure. (Is that a definition of
integrity?) Teach me today from the life of Joseph.

Everyone could see it—Joseph was a star on the rise, a born leader and
beautiful to behold. No wonder the mistress of the house wanted him.
Little did she know that Pharaoh himself would soon be begging for the
young man's attention (Gen. 41:41). But Joseph belonged to You.

Show me the power of integrity, Lord. Especially in those areas
where You've gifted me, help me resolutely leave ownership with You.
Show me how to stand and fight to protect it. Show me hidden traps.

And Father, show me when I just need to run. Amen.

Compelled by Love

Christ's love compels us, because we are convinced that one died for all,
and therefore all died. And he died for all, that those who live should no
longer live for themselves but for him who died for them.

2 CORINTHIANS 5:14-15

PRAYING FROM 2 CORINTHIANS 5

Jesus, my Redeemer,

Your love saved my past from counting against me, my future from certain and eternal death, my present from being wasted. Thank You for Your compelling love!

Let Your compelling love determine who I live for today—not for myself or my need to please others, but for You who died in love for me, and rose again (v. 15).

Let Your compelling love change how I see others around me—no one from outward appearances alone, but everyone from the world-changing fact of Your life, death, and resurrection (v. 16).

Let Your compelling love help me remember that each person who has received Christ, including me, is a radically new creation. "The past is finished and gone, everything has become fresh and new" (v. 17, Phillips). May this new life gush out in every thought, attitude, word, and deed today. (Why do "old" when I've been re-created "new"?)

Yes, let Your compelling love sweep me up in this incredible life-work and privileged role You've called me to: ambassador of Your forgiving, healing, redeeming love to everyone I meet (vv. 18-20).

This is my prayer, dear Redeemer. I love You. And I give You permission to compel me by Your love all day long. Amen.

The Riches of Contentment

I have learned the secret of being content in any and every situation.

PHILIPPIANS 4:12

PRAYING FROM PHILIPPIANS 4

Lord,

You promise peace and contentment because You know how much we need it. How I want You to train my heart now to receive these inner riches (they're not available in any store).

Yes, I want to learn the secret of joy today. Excavate my heart to have room to receive it (kick out every impostor); redirect my attentions (away from every phony priority); tutor me to celebrate it (I've been practicing the wrong skills); shape my attitudes to express it always.

Always! Yes, I'll say it again for my own ears, because rejoicing continually in You is *normal* for believers (even when we're in trouble). May exactly this kind of irrepressible confidence in You sweeten my life and quietly prepare me for Your coming (vv. 4-5).

Right now, Lord, I release to You all worries and fears, especially about _____. For every anxious thought I put down, I pick up a prayer of childlike trust in you (v. 6). Ah, contentment!

Instead of letting anxiety hold me captive, help me pray honestly, mixing every wail of need with a generous dose of thanksgiving. Then your divine peace—a miracle completely beyond my understanding—will set a guard on my thoughts and feelings (vv. 6-7).

Save me from patterns of useless, harmful thinking. Redirect my mind toward what is excellent and praiseworthy; these bear the finger-prints of Your presence in my life (v. 8).

What excellent and praiseworthy things are You accomplishing in my life right now? I'll name them in praise to You: _____, _____, and _____. Thank You!

Lord, You are "excellent and praiseworthy." As my mind embraces You—expectantly waiting on Your redeeming work in me and my family—I will be changed. I will know true peace, no matter what the circumstance (vv. 9-12). And I will sing in my heart all day: "I am ready for anything through the strength of the One who lives within me" (v. 13, Phillips)!

Amen.

A Good Word

Who is the man who desires life, and loves length of days that he may see good? Keep your tongue from evil, and your lips from speaking deceit.

PSALM 34:12-13, NASB

Lord Jesus,

The tongue is such an unimpressive body part, but oh how much trouble it can get me into if I don't learn to master it (James 3:5)!

Today, I pray that I will speak kindly about others (Titus 3:2). Make me quick to speak only healing words (Col. 4:6). Help me not repeat negative comments (even though they make me feel powerful or in-the-know). Show me that it's not only wrong to find pleasure in others' mistakes, but it's wrong even to listen to such talk (1 Cor. 13:6; Eph. 5:11-12). Without an audience, a gossiper gives up; like a flame without air, an unrepeated rumor simply goes out (Prov. 26:20).

Help me to learn that though gossip may seem harmless, the words hurt both as I say and hear them (Prov. 18:8). Help me instead to be more like You—full of mercy (Heb. 2:17), humble (Phil. 2:8), a defender of folks in a mess (John 8:1-11).

You are my defender and advocate, always putting in a good word for me before the Father (1 John 2:1; Rom. 8:34; Heb. 7:25). When Satan comes to gossip and accuse, You deflect his hate and shield me with Your divine love and perfect record (Rev. 12:10; 1 Cor. 1:30). Thank You!

That's the kind of "good word" I want to speak all day long— words that always protect, always trust, always hope, always persevere (1 Cor. 13:7).

Amen.

Morning Conversation

In the morning I lay my requests before you and wait in expectation.

PSALM 5:3

SEEKER: From the ends of the earth I call to You, I call as my heart grows faint (Ps. 61:1-2).

LORD: *Call to Me and I will answer you and tell you great and unsearchable things you do not know* (Jer. 33:3).

SEEKER: Let the morning bring me word of Your unfailing love, for I have put my trust in You (Ps. 143:8).

LORD: *I have loved you with an everlasting love* (Jer. 31:3).

SEEKER: The enemy pursues me, he crushes me to the ground; he makes me dwell in darkness like those long dead. So my spirit grows faint within me; my heart within me is dismayed (Ps. 143:3-4).

LORD: *Trust in Me at all times. Pour out your heart before Me; I am a refuge for you* (from Ps. 62:8).

SEEKER: I am in desperate need; rescue me from those who pursue me, for they are too strong for me (Ps. 142:6).

LORD: *Be still, and know that I am God.... I will be exalted in the earth* (Ps. 46:10).

SEEKER: Ah, Sovereign LORD, You have made the heavens and the earth by Your great power and outstretched arm. Nothing is too hard for you (Jer. 32:17).

LORD: *What is impossible with men is possible with God* (Luke 18:27).

SEEKER: I love You, Lord, because You heard me (from Ps. 116:1).

LORD: *So do not fear, for I am with you; do not be dismayed, for I am your God. I will strengthen you and help you; I will uphold you with my righteous right hand* (Isa. 41:10).

Mustard–Seed Prayer

The kingdom of heaven is like a mustard seed, which a man took and planted in his field. Though it is the smallest of all your seeds, yet when it grows, it is the largest of garden plants and becomes a tree, so that the birds of the air come and perch in its branches.

MATTHEW 13:31-32

Heavenly Father,

Here are the seed-specks of faith I want to plant today:

—my active faith in Your love and power (Ps. 62:11-12)

—my settled confidence in Your saving work in my life (1 Pet. 1:3-9)

—my weaknesses, embarrassing to me but useful to You (Heb. 11:34)

—my strengths and abilities, all received from You (Rom. 12:3-8)

—my desire to know You better (Phil. 3:10-11)

—my powers of self-discipline, wavering as they are (2 Tim. 1:7)

—my time and money, as I yield to Your ownership (2 Cor. 9:6-7)

—my selfish, dying grip on "life" exchanged for the cross You offer (Matt. 16:24-26)

These are the mustard seeds I want to put in the ground for You. So tiny. So easy to misplace or misjudge. What is my "planting soil" today? A hard choice? Following through? Letting go? Sacrifice?

Show me my kingdom-planting work, and grant me faith. (It all seems so improbable.)

I assure you that if you have faith the size of a mustard-seed you can say to this hill, "Up you get and move over there!" and it will move—you will find nothing is impossible (Matt. 17:20, Phillips).

Thank You, Lord. From these tiny seeds, grow a giant faith in me! Amen.

What Do You See?

[Esther] instructed [her servant] to say to Mordecai, "All the king's officials and the people...know that for any man or woman who approaches the king in the inner court without being summoned the king has but one law: that he be put to death. The only exception to this is for the king to extend the gold scepter to him and spare his life. But thirty days have passed since I was called to go to the king." When Esther's words were reported to Mordecai, he sent back this answer: "Do not think that because you are in the king's house you alone of all the Jews will escape. For if you remain silent at this time, relief and deliverance for the Jews will arise from another place.... Who knows but that you have come to royal position for such a time as this?" Then Esther sent this reply to Mordecai: "Go, gather together all the Jews...and fast for me. Do not eat or drink for three days, night or day. I and my maids will fast as you do. When this is done, I will go to the king, even though it is against the law. And if I perish, I perish."

ESTHER 4:10-16

Heavenly Father,

Xerxes chose young Esther as his next queen because she was gorgeous, "lovely in form and features" (Esther 2:7). But You saw in her something that could stop a carefully plotted genocide in its tracks.

What do You see in me that others might be missing? What talents, interests, passions do You want me to put to work today? You've brought me to this place, to these people and these challenges for such a time as this. Thank You that You're still at work today making history through available people (Eph. 3:20; Heb. 12:1-2).

Like Esther, I want to be courageously available to You. Amen.

Building the Walls

Like a city whose walls are broken down is a man who lacks self-control.

PROVERBS 25:28

Lord,

Your Word teaches that when we truly experience Your saving grace, we find the power to say no to wasteful, worldly passions and to live self-controlled and productive lives (Titus 2:11-12). Thank You, Lord, that it's Your goodness, not Your force, that wins and keeps us in Your way (Rom 2:4).

But sometimes I need a little force to corral my laziness or self-indulgence, to bar the door against corrupting influences that sour me to Your truths, to make me do what I don't want to do at all.

Teach me and change me, Lord. I want to become more self-controlled. I don't want to let the world dominate my behavior. This is my plea, Lord: Transform me by the renewing of my mind so that I can both know and do Your good, pleasing, and perfect will (Rom. 12:2).

All around I see the devastation of a culture that says, "Anything goes," "Follow your heart," and "Just do it!" Self-indulgence is the drug of choice on every corner. But it's poison for Your children. And its main ingredient is "self."

If anyone would come after me, he must deny himself and take up his cross and follow me (Matt. 16:24).

Yes, Lord, my "self" belongs to You. It's nailed to the cross with You, along with all its passions and desires (Gal. 5:24). I relinquish ownership again today of that stinking carcass, that dark impostor, that thief of my new life in You. Since I live by Your Spirit, help me to keep in step with Your Spirit today (v. 25).

Do you not know that in a race all the runners run, but only one gets the prize? Run in such a way as to get the prize (1 Cor. 9:24).

Yes, Lord, I want the prize of Your favor and blessing today. You promise to live powerfully through me. Now show me how to build the walls of will power and restraint around my life:

—the ability to think clearly and pray effectively (1 Pet. 1:13; 4:7)

—restraint of my temper, my tongue, and all other self-indulgent reactions that so quickly get out of hand (and turn me into a fool) (Prov. 29:11)

—the privilege and honor of being treated like Your child, one who is led lovingly in paths of discipline and holy living (Heb. 12:7,10)

Thank You that I'm not defenseless—either in the face of my own weaknesses or from outside attacks. *God did not give us a spirit of timidity, but a spirit of power, of love and of self-discipline* (2 Tim. 1:7).

Powerful Lord, may the city of my life be beautiful for You today. Amen.

God's Math

When Jesus looked up and saw a great crowd coming toward him, he said to Philip, "Where shall we buy bread for these people to eat?" He asked this only to test him, for he already had in mind what he was going to do. Philip answered him, "Eight months' wages would not buy enough bread for each one to have a bite!"

JOHN 6:5-7

Lord Jesus,

It seems like You wired my brain in numeral code. In the symmetry of mathematics I see Your infinite mind at work and understand the universe You've made. When all else gets fuzzy, one plus one still equals two.

I recognize myself in Philip—any idiot could see that he was right. But today I'm asking You to teach me another way. You hold together the planets and every living thing by the Word of Your power (Heb. 1:3). Help me learn the miracle math of heaven:

Paul's Wealth Index. Godliness + contentment = continuously expanding net gain (1 Tim. 6:6).

Dr. Luke's Diagnosis. Eleven scared disciples + one Holy Spirit = eleven fearless apostles + three thousand new believers (Acts 2).

Isaiah's Double Theorem. A repentant heart + accepting God's gift = salvation for eternity. And: A quiet spirit + trust in God's power = strength for today (Isa. 30:15).

The Power Paradox. If I'm weak, then I'm strong (2 Cor. 12:10).

Lord God, You have counted every hair on my head (Matt. 10:30) and named all the stars (Isa. 40:26). Yet You live in mystery: God the Father + God the Son + God the Holy Spirit = One.

Forgive me for mistrusting or ignoring the new math of the spiritual world when I calculate what's true or worthwhile in life. I don't want to be so arrogant about linear logic that I miss the facts as You see them today.

Andrew...spoke up, "Here is a boy with five small barley loaves and two small fish, but how far will they go among so many?"

Jesus said, "Have the people sit down." There was plenty of grass in that place, and the men sat down, about five thousand of them. Jesus then took the loaves, gave thanks, and distributed to those who were seated as much as they wanted. He did the same with the fish.

When they had all had enough to eat, he said to his disciples, "Gather the pieces that are left over. Let nothing be wasted." So they gathered them and filled twelve baskets with the pieces of the five barley loaves left over by those who had eaten (John 6:8-13).

Lord Jesus, I am that boy. Here are my loaves and fish. I can't wait to see what You will do with numbers today.

Amen.

Faith Like Oxygen

Faith is being sure of what we hope for and certain of what we do not see. This is what the ancients were commended for. By faith we understand that the universe was formed at God's command, so that what is seen was not made out of what was visible.

HEBREWS 11:1-3

PRAYING FROM HEBREWS 11

Lord,

Today I pray for Your favor. I want to please You. I want my life to add up to something, both now and in eternity.

Teach me about faith, the invisible ingredient of success. Everywhere else I turn, I get other advice for how to achieve: "Get in shape," "Wear the right perfume," "Go to the right college," "Plug in to the best network."

All those plans I can see and touch and measure. But faith is more like oxygen: I can't go on without it, but I can't exactly hold it in my hands either. Lord, help me to live my life today so that I can be commended by You (v. 2).

Lead me, Holy Spirit, as I meditate on the Bible's heroes of faith: *By faith Enoch...pleased God* (v. 5). How could I please You, Lord? Through a vibrant faith in You, help me to act with justice, to love mercy in all my relationships, and to walk humbly with You (Mic. 6:8).

By faith Noah...in holy fear built an ark to save his family (v. 7). How can I live in holy fear of You, Lord? By trusting in Your character, help me to hold You in awe and reverence as I should—that's the first step in every wise, secure choice (Prov. 1:7; 14:26).

By faith Abraham, when called to go…obeyed and went (v. 8). How can I obey You, Lord? Through the eyes of faith, show me that Your will for me is my heritage forever and the true joy of my life (Ps. 119:111).

By faith Jacob…worshiped (v. 21). How can I worship You, Lord? With a heart changed by a spiritual rebirth, help me to praise and exalt You no matter what difficult circumstances might shake me today (Heb. 12:28-29).

By faith Moses…chose to be mistreated along with the people of God rather than to enjoy the pleasures of sin for a short time (vv. 24-25). How can I endure persecution and even shame with Your people today? Through radical belief in what You're up to in this world, help me to accept opposition as a gift, and part of my true calling as a disciple of Jesus (Phil. 1:29; 1 Pet. 2:21).

I come to You today believing that You exist, and that You graciously and faithfully reward those who earnestly seek You (Heb. 11:6). I do long to please You, Lord, and in some way to become a hero in Your family of faith.

Do not throw away your confidence; it will be richly rewarded…. My righteous one will live by faith (Heb. 10:35,38).

Yes, Lord. Let it be so today.

Amen.

Angel Warriors

The angel of the LORD encamps around those who fear him, and he delivers them.

PSALM 34:7

Lord of angels,
Thank You for Your heavenly beings with which You surround my life. These guardians take a stand for Your kingdom in the unseen realm every day (Eph. 6:12). Today, when I think that what's in front of my nose or what I can see or touch is all that matters, remind me of the reality of that other dimension.

My angels are ministering spirits sent to serve those who will inherit My salvation (from Heb. 1:14).

Open my understanding to "spiritual forces" (Eph. 6:12). I don't want to be ignorant or vulnerable. Yet I thank You that I can trust in You and Your "ministering spirits." Your angel warriors can shut the mouths of lions and defeat any agent of Satan (Ps. 103:20; Dan. 6:22).

If you make Me your refuge, then no disaster will overwhelm you. I will command My angels to guard you and your children in all your ways (from Ps. 91:9-12).

Thank You that Your angels of mercy and power guard me and those I love. Even the weakest is safe with You.

See that you do not look down on one of these little ones. For I tell you that their angels in heaven always see the face of My Father in heaven (Matt. 18:10).

When I'm afraid today, help me to remember my angels, just beyond my sight. They're on guard—right here, right now. Thank You! Amen.

Heart Full of Holes

He heals the brokenhearted and binds up their wounds.

Dear Lord,

I come to You today with a heart full of holes and the wind blowing through. My hopes are in tatters; my spirit broods over my life like a bird of prey circling above burned-out ruins (Ps. 102:6).

Something's lost. Scattered. Lying in pieces all around me. Someone's hurtful or hurting. Broken or breaking. Going, going, gone…

Jesus, You know all about heartbreak: You were called "a man of sorrows and familiar with suffering" (Isa. 53:3). Breathe Your healing presence into my being, O Lord. I lift up my soul to You (Ps. 86:4).

You said, "Blessed are those who mourn, for they will be comforted" (Matt. 5:4). Blessed, You said.

Blessed? Then bless me, Lord. Touch me, gentle Savior. Carry me, Father of compassion and God of all comfort (2 Cor. 1:3).

In the midst of your sorrow, the Lord is giving you seeds for a harvest. If you go forward now, sowing in tears, you will return with songs of joy, bringing abundance with you (from Ps. 126:4-6).

Blessing? Harvest? Songs of joy? Help me trust You with my tears today. Because You understand. And because, in Your hands, every grief is the seed for joy and bounty later. It's something only You can do. (You must drive Satan crazy!)

Jesus, I pray in Your name.

Amen.

Baffling Choices

The men sat down, about five thousand of them. Jesus then took the loaves, gave thanks, and distributed to those who were seated as much as they wanted. He did the same with the fish. When they had all had enough to eat, he said to his disciples, "Gather the pieces that are left over. Let nothing be wasted." So they gathered them and filled twelve baskets with the pieces of the five barley loaves left over by those who had eaten. After the people saw the miraculous sign that Jesus did, they began to say, "Surely this is the Prophet who is to come into the world." Jesus, knowing that they intended to come and make him king by force, withdrew again to a mountain by himself.

JOHN 6:10-15

Lord Jesus,

Because You turned down a promotion—one that You deserved (You are, after all, the King of kings), one that could have spared You hunger, shame, weakness, and death; and because You never forgot Your real mission on earth, and were unwilling to compromise it…

I pray to You with confidence today about baffling choices I face at work. Especially, I bring to You _____. And these people whose opinions and decisions are critical to my success: _____ and _____ and _____. Your Word says praise tests a person and that any successful venture requires wisdom and knowledge (Prov. 27:21; 24:3). Help me find the facts, sort through my pride issues, and know what to do.

Seek God's kingdom first and his righteousness, and all that you need will be given you as well (from Matt. 6:33).

Thank You, my Lord and King.

Amen.

Seeing the Invisible

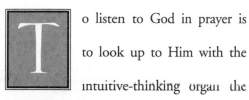o listen to God in prayer is to look up to Him with the intuitive-thinking organ the Bible calls the heart. Through the eyes and the ears of the heart we see and hear God; through it we apprehend the transcendent— that which is beyond the merely physical or material. The Scriptures graciously invite us to look up and see the invisible.

LEANNE PAYNE

Under His Wings

He will cover you with his feathers, and under his wings you will find refuge; His faithfulness will be your shield and rampart.

PSALM 91:4

PRAYING PSALM 91

Dear Father God,

I pray today for Your protection. You know the very real illnesses, violence, and accidents we face every day. And You know how some days just the possibility of these dangers shakes my confidence.

Help me to remember today who You are—"Most High," "Almighty," and "my God, in whom I trust" (vv. 1-2). Your goodness and power are my constant shield. Thank You, Father. Be a place of safety for my family and the loved ones You've placed in my life. Cover us from above like an eagle spreading her wings over her chicks (v. 4). As we trust in Your care, take away the fears that grip us in the night, the worries that nag us by day (v. 5). Set a barrier of safety around us— like the stone walls of a fortress—keeping out injury, disease, accident, and crime (v. 6). Place Your shining angels by our side all day long, shielding us from spiritual or physical attack because we belong to You (vv. 11-12). Thank You, loving and powerful Lord!

Today, I pray especially for the protection of _____. You are his/her true home and eternal refuge.

Because she loves me, I will protect her, for she acknowledges my name. I will answer her. I will be with her in trouble (from vv. 14-15).

Thank you, Mighty God!

Amen.

Praying the Ten Commandments

Be careful to do what the LORD your God has commanded you; do not turn aside to the right or to the left. Walk in all the way that the LORD your God has commanded you, so that you may live and prosper and prolong your days.

DEUTERONOMY 5:32-33

Lord God,

You asked us to etch Your commands in our memories and affections, and to do the same for our children (Deut. 6:6-7). I pray today for myself, for all who are close to me, and for all believers. Show us, Lord, what it really means to fear You and keep your laws. We want to honor You and receive the best life has to offer (Deut. 7:12).

1. *I am the LORD your God, who brought you out of...slavery. You shall have no other gods before me* (Deut. 5:6-7). May no other loyalties or affections take Your place in our hearts—no other priority, hobby, ambition, possession, or person. We belong to only You!

2. *You shall not make for yourself an idol in the form of anything in heaven above or on the earth beneath.... You shall not...worship them; for I...am a jealous God* (vv. 8-9). Help us to resist any substitute objects of worship (how easily idols slip in!) and to turn away from all false beliefs. Keep us from any pursuit—no matter how worthy—that becomes an end in itself.

3. *You shall not misuse the name of the LORD your God* (v. 11). We want to hold You in awe and respect, Lord. In this casually profane world, keep us sensitive about the sacredness of Your names, especially "Lord," "God," and "Jesus Christ."

4. *Observe the Sabbath day by keeping it holy* (vv. 12-15). May we faithfully set aside the Lord's day for worship and rest, and for nurturing a vital role in Your church family. Thank You for setting us free from the tyranny of work and "getting ahead."

5. *Honor your father and your mother, as the LORD your God has commanded you, so that you may live long and that it may go well with you* (v. 16). May we show lifelong respect for the elderly, especially our own parents. Help us to raise our children to respect and obey us as their main source for learning about life and godliness.

6. *You shall not murder* (v. 17). Help us to understand and guard the sanctity of all human life—including the unborn, the weak, those different from ourselves, or the aged. May we never, even in our thoughts, surrender to hate, violence, or taking revenge.

7. *You shall not commit adultery* (v. 18). May we build our marriages on integrity, purity, faithfulness, and loyalty. Protect us from the traps of pornography, promiscuity, and creeping disrespect. Show us new ways to honor marriage as a sacred, lifelong commitment.

8. *You shall not steal* (v. 19). Teach us to value honesty in the little and large issues, to respect the belongings of others (including our government and our church), and to trust You to provide for our needs.

9. *You shall not give false testimony against your neighbor* (v. 20). Instill in us a sincere dedication to being loyal and truthful, even under pressure. Teach us to hate gossip and criticism.

10. *You shall not covet* (v. 21). Help us never to measure our happiness by the lives or possessions of others. Instead, may we learn to be content with what You give and happy when others prosper.

Lord God, thank You for Your promise to bless us if we follow these laws. We want Your best to be the measure of our lives (7:12).

Amen.

All God's Children

The Spirit himself testifies with our spirit that we are God's children.

ROMANS 8:16

PROMISES FOR YOUR DAY

Our Privilege

Because _____ has believed Jesus Christ and accepted him,
the Lord has given _____ the right to become a child of God.
(from John 1:12, NLT)

Our Guiding Light

All who are led by the Spirit of God
are children of God.
(Rom. 8:14, NLT)

Our Comfort

As a mother comforts her child,
so You, Lord, will comfort _____ today.
(from Isa. 66:13)

Our Family Name

How great is the love the Father has lavished on _____,
that he/she should be called a child of God.
And that's exactly what he is!
(from 1 John 3:1)

That Was Close!

He has saved me from death, my eyes from tears, my feet from stumbling.
I shall live! Yes, in his presence—here on earth!

PSALM 116:8-9, TLB

PRAYING PSALM 116

I love You, Lord!
I love You because You heard my cry for help and mercifully answered (v. 1). And because You turned Your ear to me, I will keep calling to You as long as I live (v. 2).

Oh, the end seemed so close! Trouble and sorrow held me under. Death had me by the throat. But You heard me calling out, "O Lord, save me!" And You answered (vv. 3-4). Thank You!

You are full of grace, Lord. You are good all through. You are overflowing in compassion—even for one as foolish and needy and accident-prone as I am (vv. 5-6). Thank You!

How can I repay you, Lord, for Your salvation (v. 12)?

—Rest in Him—surrender completely to the inevitability of His prevailing goodness (v. 7).

—Tell others about the reality of His saving power (v. 13).

—Be thankful (v. 17).

—Keep my promises to Him (v. 18).

Yes, I do love You, Lord! Let me live to obey—and keep on praising You.

Amen.

Right, Left, Stop, Go

I will instruct you and teach you in the way which you should go;
I will counsel you with My eye upon you.

PSALM 32:8, NASB

Lord,

Open the way ahead. I can't make the right decisions without You. But
You are the Lord Almighty, wonderful in counsel and magnificent in
wisdom (Isa. 28:29).

I'm not asking for magic, Lord. You've given me abilities and infor-
mation and motivation—help me to put all of it to work today. But
when I get lost because of ignorance or wrong motives, mercifully intervene. Nudge me in the right direction by that still, small voice that says,
left, right, stop, go back, or go straight on (Isa. 30:19-21). By Your
Spirit, guide me as You've promised (John 16:13).

In my close relationships today, I pray for specific direction about
_____. And for challenges I face on the job, I pray specifically
about _____. All day, Lord, I'll listen for Your counsel, how-
ever it might come to me.

I will lead the blind by ways you have not known, along unfamiliar
paths I will guide you. I will turn the darkness into light before you and
make the rough places smooth. These are the things I will do; I will not for-
sake you (from Isa. 42:16).

Thank you, Lord. I have every reason to trust You today. All day,
may my attitude of quiet expectation flow back to You as the expression
of my sincere worship (Isa. 30:15).

Amen.

Race to Win

*In a race all the runners run, but only one gets the prize. Run in such a
way as to get the prize.*

1 CORINTHIANS 9:24

Lord,

You've asked me to race away from some things—"flee" the love of
money, false beliefs, and malicious talk, for example (1 Tim. 6:3-11).
And You've asked me to race toward others—"pursue" righteousness,
godliness, faith, love, endurance, and gentleness (v. 11).

Help me run fast today. By Your grace and power, and my commitment, I want to compete in the race of faith and take hold of the eternal life You bestowed when I confessed You as my Lord (v. 12).

Today I see the crowds of onlookers in the bleachers—my parents,
my elders in the faith, the generations of Your followers who have gone
before. May their example spur me to press on (Heb. 12:1).

Please help me to throw off everything that holds me back or
diverts my energies—bad habits, temptations, laziness, wrong priorities.
Deliver me, Lord, from the sin that so easily entangles my mind, my
hands, and my feet. Help me to run strong and true down the track
You've marked out as mine (Heb. 12:1).

But effort isn't enough. Even good intentions. Only the blue ribbon
will do. Lord, help me to run so as to win (1 Cor. 9:24)!

Your approval and Your loving presence for eternity are the only
prizes that matter. Any other wins are only losses (Phil. 3:7-8)!

Today, help me to keep my back turned toward every past failure
and to press on toward the finish line—to win (Phil. 3:13-14).

Amen.

Prince of Peace

You will keep in perfect peace him whose mind is steadfast, because he trusts in you.

ISAIAH 26:3

Lord Jesus,

I pray today for personal peace. Anxieties rise up like the tide to swamp me. Worries seep in, especially when I'm alone. My thoughts are troubled, stirred up like a shallow bay in a squall. But You quieted the wind and the waves.

Peace I leave with you; my peace I give you.... Do not let your hearts be troubled and do not be afraid (John 14:27). Thank You, Lord, for Your gift of peace. I receive it now.

In this world you will have trouble. But take heart! I have overcome the world (John 16:33). Oh, how I let the raw blasts of the world get inside and toss around my soul, chill my confidence, turn over my trust, and whistle in my ears till I can hardly hear You. How I need a lasting, worshipful awareness of Your nearness today. Help me to shut out the gales. Teach me how to overcome the world of cares.

I have told you these things so that in me you may have peace (John 16:33). Yes, I listen to You today, Lord. I listen and receive. Please rule in my heart, Prince of peace (Isa. 9:6; Col. 3:15).

Do not be anxious about anything, but in everything, by prayer and petition, with thanksgiving, tell me your requests. And My peace, which transcends all understanding, will guard your hearts and your minds (from Phil. 4:6-7). Thank You, Lord. I'll tell You everything. I'll trust You with the outcomes. And I'll rest in Your serene presence.

Amen.

Tactical Surrenders

You have heard that it was said, "Love your neighbor and hate your enemy." But I tell you: Love your enemies and pray for those who persecute you, that you may be sons of your Father in heaven.

MATTHEW 5:43-45

Dear Lord Jesus,

What I wanted was Your help to do my life the way I please: extra power now and then, rock-solid guarantees, more bliss, more wins...

What do You mean love my enemies? Bless those who are trying to suck the life out of me?

Like the disciples, I respond to Your command today with a gasp (Matt. 19:25). Who can do such a thing? And yet...

—You loved those who deserted You (John 21:15-19).

—You forgave those who tortured and killed You (Luke 23:34).

—You said, "Forgive, so you can receive forgiveness" (Matt. 6:12).

—You said if someone steals something from you, let him take more; if she hurts you, let her hurt you again; if they persecute you, ask God to pour out His best gifts on them (Matt. 5:40-42; Rom. 12:14).

—You didn't say, "Get the winner's edge," but, "Deny yourself, take up your cross, and follow me" (Mark 8:34).

Unless I see with the eyes of the Spirit, Your teachings will only seem like a quick way to lose. So penetrate my heart today, radical Lord. Turn the glaring light of Your subversive love onto my often self-justifying, small, and vengeful spirit. Peel my fingers off the scoreboard (that's Your business) (Rom. 12:19). Help me learn the freedom of forgiveness and the surprising blessings of praying for those who oppose me.

Amen.

Anselm's Prayer for His Enemies

lmighty and tender Lord Jesus Christ,

Just as I have asked you to love my friends, so I ask the same for my enemies.

You alone, Lord, are mighty. You alone are merciful.

Whatever you make me desire for my enemies, give it to them. And give the same back to me.

If I ever ask for them anything which is outside your perfect rule of love, whether through weakness, ignorance or malice, Good Lord, do not give it to them, and do not give it back to me.

When Love Is Hard

This is the message you heard from the beginning: We should love one another.

1 JOHN 3:11

Heavenly Father,

Sometimes the hardest place to love is at home, and the hardest ones to love are the ones we love most. On days when irritations, grudges, or weariness threaten to sabotage my closest relationships, bring a healing presence. Where You are is love (1 John 4:12). Be here.

By Your love working through me, and my willingness to give when it hurts, help me to love at all times. That's the measure of true friendship (Prov. 17:17). May my caring go far past the convenience of nice sentiments—"I wish you well; keep warm and well fed"—and accomplish actual good with sincere actions (James 2:17; 1 John 3:18).

Father, grow love—be love—in me; share the beauty of Your love in all its colors. As Your chosen child today, I want to be clothed with:

—compassion (to try to understand the other person's experience)

—kindness (to show generosity and goodwill)

—humility (to remember my own shortcomings)

—gentleness (to respect each other's sensitivities)

—patience (to value what only time can accomplish) (Col. 3:12)

Especially help me to be forbearing with "difficult" people, forgiving whatever grievances I may have against them—just as Christ has forgiven me (Col. 3:13).

In Jesus' name I pray. Amen.

Magnum Opus

We are God's workmanship, created in Christ Jesus to do good works, which God prepared in advance for us to do.

EPHESIANS 2:10

Heavenly Father,

How amazing that You consider me a work of art in Your creation gallery. Somehow I get focused on my flaws or sins, but You call me Your special "work-in-progress." What a creation miracle I am, Lord! I will exalt You today because, in perfect faithfulness, You are accomplishing supernatural things in my life, things planned long ago (Isa. 25:1).

Like the farthest star and tiniest flower on Creation Day, I am the skilled, caring work of Your fingers. How excellent is Your name in all the earth (Ps. 8:1)! Thank You that when Your personal, loving intentions for me are realized, You will exclaim again, "It is very good!" (Gen.1:31).

Yes, everything You imagine and shape is good (Ps. 119:68). How grateful I am that Your unchanging goodness will surround me, and be at work in me, my whole life (Ps. 23:6).

Thank You that what You have started in my life, You will certainly finish. And when I stand in Christ's presence, I will look amazingly like Him (Phil. 1:6; 1 John 3:2). What a longed-for miracle that will be!

Until that celebration day, breathe into my heart and soul both the will and the power to seek and serve You, and to wait patiently while You work (Phil. 2:13).

In Jesus' name I pray. Amen.

Working It Out

Be strong and courageous, and do the work. Do not be afraid or
discouraged, for the LORD God, my God, is with you. He will not fail
you or forsake you until all the work…is finished.

1 CHRONICLES 28:20

Lord God,

I know you have put me in this job, this family, this place and time for
a reason. Even the challenges that make me want to complain or quit or
doubt Your involvement are part of Your big plan. Every trouble is just
another opportunity for You to triumph! Thank You!

Touch my emotions and my will this morning through Your Word.
I want to be a workman for You who doesn't need to be ashamed of my
attitudes and my performance (2 Tim. 2:15).

You've chosen me to work for You. David told Solomon that God had
chosen him to build the temple (1 Chron. 28:6) with plans the Spirit
had provided (v. 12). Solomon's first job was to bring the right attitude
to the task: "And you, my son Solomon, acknowledge the God of your
father, and serve him with wholehearted devotion and with a willing
mind, for the LORD searches every heart and understands every motive
behind the thoughts…. For the LORD has chosen you to build a
temple as a sanctuary. Be strong and do the work" (vv. 9-10).

Thank You for choosing me, too, Father. I acknowledge You as my
God—owner, boss, ultimate judge, and Lord. Help me to do my work
today with enthusiasm, single-mindedness, and right motives. I choose
for myself what You have chosen for me today.

You'll help me learn the rules of success at work. When he led the

Israelites in the formidable task of rebuilding Jerusalem after the captivity, Nehemiah depended on prayer (Neh. 1:5-11; 4:4-5) and preparation (4:12-23). The results spoke for themselves: "When all our enemies heard about this [the completed city walls], the surrounding nations were afraid and lost their self-confidence, because they realized that this work had been done with the help of our God" (Neh. 6:16).

Yes, Lord, let the events of today overwhelm every person or force that opposes what You're trying to accomplish in and through me. Make my enemies look like what they are—losers! Because You are the real power at work here. Teach me to do my part so You can do Your part. I want to pray diligently and prepare wisely, creatively, and thoroughly.

You've asked me to persevere in my work. Called to be a missionary, Paul wrote that his daily duties made him look like a fool and a spectacle (1 Cor. 4:9-10): "To this very hour we go hungry and thirsty, we are in rags, we are brutally treated, we are homeless. We work hard with our own hands. When we are cursed, we bless; when we are persecuted, we endure it; when we are slandered, we answer kindly" (vv. 11-13).

Lord, forgive me for whining about my "trials." Bless me with the perseverance of Paul to serve you in little and large ways today. Press his encouragement into my heart: "Therefore, my dear brothers, stand firm. Let nothing move you. Always give yourselves fully to the work of the Lord, because you know that your labor in the Lord is not in vain" (1 Cor. 15:58).

Help me to go about every task today as Jesus did, whose only wish was to bring You glory (John 17:4). May Your favor rest upon us. Make the work of our hands today count for eternity—yes, make it count, Lord (Ps. 90:17)!

In Jesus' name I pray. Amen.

Look Away

Remove your scourge from me; I am overcome by the blow of your hand.... Look away from me, that I may rejoice again.

PSALM 39:10,13

PRAYING FROM PSALM 42

All-seeing Lord,
Look away from me today. Your love feels too much like pain. Your protection weighs me down like chain-mail armor. Your discipline seems to push me farther and farther away from You.

Put your hope in God, for I will yet praise him, my Savior and my God (Ps. 42:11).

Right now, I don't feel hope. What I feel is exhaustion, aches, water in my ears. "All your waves and breakers have swept over me" (v. 7). Look away, merciful God. Your ever-present gaze is too much like an invasion, like a question I can't answer.

Put your hope in God, for I will yet praise him, my Savior and my God.

I remember music, singing, happy days. I was the one leading the procession to celebrate good times and a good God (v. 4). But the only ones singing today are those who don't care about You or Your existence, much less living a life that pleases You (vv. 9-10).

Put your hope in God, for I will yet praise him, my Savior and my God.

I am in pain and distress, O God (Ps. 69:29). But could You receive my struggle as a kind of acknowledgment, my weariness as a clue that I do care? Could You even protect me from my own prayer?
Amen.

Keeping Company with God

f we want to keep company with God, we must be prepared to let him remind us of his ways, not at the times that suit us, but at the times that suit him. If, through our use of the Bible, through our reading and meditation, we let him into our hearts, below the level of our deliberation, that means that we hand over to him the right to choose how and when to present himself to our consciousness. We all like keeping God in a cupboard with the best china and the family silver, to look at when we feel inclined. But the living God chooses his own times, and will come when he is not wanted.

SIMON TUGWELL

Tests of Time

There is a time for everything, and a season for every activity under heaven.

PRAYING FROM ECCLESIASTES 3

Lord of time and eternity,
Somewhere in my mind, a voice is always whispering lies about the clock: that tomorrow will never come; that when it does, it'll be just like today; that I have all the time in the world...

Teach me to number my days carefully and wisely (Ps. 90:12).

In *a time to be born* (v. 2)...remind me that You are the only Creator. By the word of Your power (2 Pet. 3:5), You can make new life spring up—in humans, in careers, in relationships, in commitments.

In *a time to die* (v. 2)...comfort me in my loss. Help me and those I love to reach in faith to Jesus, the Resurrection and the Life (John 11:25).

In *a time to plant* (v. 2)...give me seeds of hope and perseverance. Help me to do the work You've called me to do and wait with joy for the good results You promise (1 Pet. 1:13).

In *a time to uproot* (v. 2)...help me pull up those weeds that are keeping Your best from flourishing in my life—old habits, wrong attitudes, false assumptions, compromising relationships. I never want the cares and distractions of this world to squeeze the life out of me (Luke 8:7,14).

In *a time to search* (v. 6)...for truth, or a solution to a nagging problem, for the work You have for me—grant me perseverance. You've promised to lead me through the dark to the right destination (Isa. 42:16).

In *a time to give up* (v. 6)...I ask for grace to be content with things as they are. Let satisfaction and acceptance be my riches then (1 Tim. 6:6-10).

In *a time to be silent* (v. 7)...help me to be quiet and listen (James 1:19).

In *a time to speak* (v. 7)...put Your wisdom on my tongue and Your motives in my heart. May every word be positive, building up the confidence of those around me (Prov. 15:4; 1 Pet. 4:11).

In *a time to love* (v. 8)...may I give myself to others with sincerity and abandon (Rom. 12:9).

In *a time to hate* (v. 8)...help me to reject what separates anyone from You—help me to respond quickly and decisively (Rom. 12:9).

I was born for eternity, Lord, and You'll take me there someday (Eccles. 3:11). But may each beat of my heart remind me that the clock is ticking. I have a job to do (Rom. 12:1-2), an appointment with death and judgment that may arrive at any moment (Rom. 14:10; Heb. 9:27).

By Your grace, I want to pass the tests of time today.
Amen.

Open Door, Open Heart

Offer hospitality to one another without grumbling.

1 PETER 4:9

Lord,
Today I pray for a life where the door is always open and the welcome mat is always out. People who live this way obey You and bless others in surprising ways—and sometimes meet angels (Heb. 13:1-2)!

Lord, help me value and invest in a reputation like Gaius's, the early Christian about whom almost nothing is written except that the whole church in Rome enjoyed his hospitality (Rom. 16:23). Help me to think of hospitality in terms of the unexpected gifts I can give to my guests: listening, acceptance, encouragement, laughter, friendship, beauty, grace, pleasure, delight just to be alive, or simply a change from routines. Give me a joyful zeal to be an expert at giving these lovely, overlooked gifts. Help me remember how often You touched lives around a table or in a welcoming home (Mark 14:22; Luke 19:5; 22:14; 24:30).

When guests are coming, help me not to get hung up on whether the dishes match or the house is impressive. Instead, give me the spiritual graces to know what my company might feel or need. Help me to seize the opportunity to express genuine interest in others (Phil. 2:4).

Lord, is there someone—a person, a family, a group—You're asking me to open up to today? Forgive me for saying I care while keeping my doors, my schedule, and my energies all to myself.

Amen.

The Good Fight

I have fought the good fight, I have finished the race, I have kept the faith.

2 TIMOTHY 4:7

Mighty Lord,

How much I want to fight the good fight of the faith which Paul was able to write about so confidently. Yet so often I feel like a runner with no shoes or like a boxer who's down for the count, just waiting for the bell.

Forgive me, Father, when my faith is weak, my strength is sapped, and doubts pin me to the canvas.

Today, help me to remember that You are my coach in this struggle to live by faith. You are *for* me—in my corner every moment (2 Tim. 4:17; Rom. 8:28-31)! When I stumble in temptation, Your anger lasts only a moment, but Your favor lasts a lifetime (Ps. 30:5). When I'm tired and doubting, You are my refuge and strength, an ever-present help in trouble (Ps. 46:1). And when I just can't fight a spiritual battle myself, You step in the ring and fight for me (2 Tim. 4:18)!

Today may I listen closely for Your advice in my ear. May I remember that You are not only the One who helps me to fight with faith, but You are ultimately the prize I am fighting for (1 Pet. 1:3-9).

And even when I lose a round, because of Your sweet saving grace, I still wear your Son's robes of righteousness, like a champion's robe of victory (2 Cor. 5:17,21). Thank You, Heavenly Father.

Amen.

True Wealth

Give everyone what you owe him: If you owe taxes, pay taxes; if revenue,
then revenue; if respect, then respect; if honor, then honor.

ROMANS 13:7

Lord,

Today I pray for help in the area of debt and money management. Your
Word teaches to "let no debt remain outstanding except the debt of
love" (from Rom. 13:8). And, "Do not be a man who…puts up security for debts; if you lack the means to pay, your very bed will be
snatched from under you" (Prov. 22:26-27).

I still have a bed, but how easy it is to fall into the trap of living
beyond my means.

Debt is a thief. It robs me both of money and miracles—of opportunities to see You provide for me and my family in Your own, better
way.

Strip away all my silly delusions about what money buys. Expose
those foolish desires and outright sins that drive overspending: pride,
greed, coveting, and lack of faith.

Change me, Lord.

You told Your disciples, "Much is required from those to whom
much is given" (Luke 12:48, TLB). And You've blessed me with true
wealth. Grow in me the convictions of a good steward:

—to be faithful with what You've given me

—to try to return more than what You've loaned to me

—and, with every dollar and cent spent, to bring You joy (Matt.
25:14-30)

What debt can I repay today? Help me settle my accounts with honor.

What inordinate love for material things is sabotaging the renewed life You want for me? Search my heart. Forgive me, please. Redirect my affections.

What practical step can I take right now that will move me toward freedom from debt and delusion?

Show me and help me, gracious Lord.

Amen.

The Promise by the Road

With her two [widowed] daughters-in-law [Naomi] left the place where she had been living and set out on the road that would take them back to the land of Judah.... But Naomi said, "Return home, my daughters. Why would you come with me? Am I going to have any more sons, who could become your husbands?"... But Ruth replied, "Don't urge me to leave you or to turn back from you. Where you go I will go, and where you stay I will stay. Your people will be my people and your God my God. Where you die I will die, and there I will be buried. May the LORD deal with me...if anything but death separates you and me."

RUTH 1:7,11,16-17

Heavenly Father,

Today I meditate on Ruth's story of devotion—to care for her widowed mother-in-law and to follow her newfound faith in You. She was willing to leave the familiarity of home, relatives, and language behind in Moab. She was willing to put aside her hopes for remarriage. (How would a foreigner, a hated Moabite at that, find a husband in Israel?)

Instead, she made a radical promise to invest the rest of her life in Naomi's well-being. No wonder Ruth's beautiful vow is part of so many wedding ceremonies, and no wonder You soon provided a husband for her (Ruth 4:9-10).

Lifelong vows of unqualified love are rare these days. But You honor and bless that kind of devotion—to spouse, to children, to parents, to You.

Father, I ask for help to make Ruth's beautiful, powerful, unconditional choice today.

In Jesus' name I pray. Amen.

Pray the Price

I looked for a man among them who would build up the wall and stand before me in the gap on behalf of the land so I would not have to destroy it, but I found none.

EZEKIEL 22:30

Dear Father,

Thank You for teaching me to talk to You, to tell You my needs, to respond to Your love and power, and to listen to Your Word and Your Spirit. Teach me also to pray for others.

I want to grow up in my faith and in my prayer effectiveness, to be an intercessor and "prayer partner" with the Holy Spirit for Your work in this world. Thank You that Jesus is the Man in the gap for me— always interceding on my behalf in Your presence (Rom. 8:34). How I praise You, my God!

Show me what people and what causes You're putting in my "prayer portfolio" today: Children? Spouse? Coworkers? My pastor or others I know in ministry? Those in positions of authority and influence? Ones who seem caught in illness or destructive behavior? Enemies of Christ?

I want to take my place in the gap. I want to excel at "giving prayers," not just "gimme prayers." Help me to nurture a growing sincerity and tenacity to be a "prayer striver"—the kind Paul so valued in his missionary work (Rom 15:30). This prayer work is my duty, but I accept it as my privilege and opportunity, too.

Mentor me, interceding Spirit, to "pray the price":

—like Daniel, to pray diligently and regularly, no matter what kind of outward or inward opposition I face (Dan. 6:10);

—like Samuel, to understand that to fail in this calling for those You put in my care is a sin (1 Sam. 12:23);

—like the widow before the judge, to persist in my requests, knowing that You've promised to answer if I don't give up (Luke 18:1-7).

May the requests I make for others be nonjudgmental, humble, and from a pure heart because these are the qualities of spiritual conversation You most highly esteem (James 5:16; Isa. 57:15).

Thank You so much for those loving and faithful ones who've prayed for me in my life. As they have blessed me, bless them lavishly today!

In Jesus' name. Amen.

Birth Pangs

Intercession is coming to God on behalf of another. All intercession is prayer, but not all prayer is intercession.... A major ministry of intercessors is to bring into being the purposes of God, and many describe some of their more intense periods of intercession as travail. Mothers know even better than could the apostle Paul the full meaning of his statement, "My little children, for whom I labor in birth again until Christ is formed in you" (Gal. 4:19).

C. PETER WAGNER

Veggies with Love

Better a meal of vegetables where there is love than a fattened calf with hatred.

Gracious Lord,

Some days I realize I'm a marketer's dream—always wanting, looking, wishing I had something newer or better. Surely this unrelenting appetite is part of my old, unchanged nature that wars with Your Spirit.

I seem to be a born stuff-collector (all in the name of a great deal or impeccable taste, of course). I defend want as if it should be enshrined up there with need. And how quickly I rationalize, "But I deserve that."

Do not love the world or anything in the world.... Everything in the world—the cravings of sinful man, the lust of his eyes and the boasting of what he has and does—comes not from the Father but from the world (1 John 2:15-16).

Even my drive for personal growth can lead me astray. How easy to know, but not do; to feel conviction, but not follow through with change; to run after the latest idea, but get lazy with the changeless truths.

Your Word today is about veggies with love that become a feast. Forgive me for my discontent. Forgive me for the needless stress and waste I cause myself and others because I don't get what I want, and don't ask You for what You're ready to give (James 4:1-3).

Godliness with contentment is great gain (1 Tim. 6:6).

I know happiness never comes from more stuff in our homes (Luke 12:15) but from more life in our hearts (John 10:10). Today, I choose the beautiful simplicity of having You! Everything else is extra.

Amen.

All

And God is able to make all grace abound to you, so that in all things at all times, having all that you need, you will abound in every good work.

2 CORINTHIANS 9:8

Loving God,

I trust You to make this a day of true abundance. Before I even get out of bed, You've made available to me:

All grace. Your mercy, love, forgiveness, sufficiency, presence, faithfulness, kindness, power, and provision are mine in overflowing plenty today.

In all things. In needs, challenges, failures, obstacles, spiritual opposition, bad habits, new territory, dangerous associations, promising ventures, temptations, opportunities to witness, occasions to make amends, or any other thing that might come my way today.

At all times. In routines, emergencies, unplanned events, surprises; in crowds and alone, with friends or with antagonists; when everything's going well, when nothing is; for yesterday's regrets, for tomorrow's potential, and for whatever tests might come my way today.

Having all that I need. You've generously provided for me: physical strength, spiritual power, emotional encouragement, intellectual resources, money, help, ideas, skills, wisdom, words (even my prayers when I can't pray), and many other needs You know about but I don't today.

And all for what purpose? So that...

I may abound in every good work. Lord, I ask that Your extravagant grace to me will result today in a profusion of thoughts and activities that please You and bless others.

Thank You, generous Lord. Amen.

I Need You Now

To you I call, O LORD.... If you remain silent, I will be like those who have gone down to the pit.

PSALM 28:1

Dear Lord God,

Silence wraps around me like fog. Silence, loneliness, and confusion.

How much I want to hear Your voice today. A word. An answer. A gesture. Simply a clue that You're here with me in this stillness.

But it's dead quiet today. Have mercy on me, Lord. I'm made of dust today, not faith. I'm Your deaf child, one stumble away from the grave (Ps. 88:1-4).

Father, Abba, I'm calling to You. Please talk.

I know You've called me to a walk of faith, not sight (2 Cor. 5:7). I remember You have led me through life's deserts and across seas, often without leaving a trace of Your presence (Ps. 77:19). So in faith, dear Lord, I pray my invitation: I wait for You; my soul waits, and in the sound of Your voice I put my hope. I wait for Your voice more eagerly than a shivering watchman waits for the morning (from Ps. 130:5-6).

Answer me, O LORD, out of the goodness of your love (Ps. 69:16).

Break the silence, I pray. Or heal my ears. Maybe just say my name.

I will instruct you, and teach you in the way you should go; I will counsel you and watch over you. I have summoned you by name; _____, you are mine (Ps. 32:8; from Isa. 43:1).

Yearning

e must love God with all our power, with fear, wonder, yearning, awe. Yearn for God with great yearning.

At times this will lead us to breathless silence. I think that some of the greatest prayer is prayer when you don't utter one word or ask for anything.

A. W. TOZER

Set Me Free

You will know the truth, and the truth will set you free.

Heavenly Father,

Thank You for taking me off death row. The truth of the gospel freed me to enjoy new life in Christ (Rom. 6:18). I praise and thank You!

My prayer now is that Your truth will continue to change me, shape me, heal me. Break every chain of my old self, loving God! Set me free.

When I arrogantly slip into thinking that special rules apply to me, unmask the deception: "Do not be deceived: God cannot be mocked. A man reaps what he sows. The one who sows to please his sinful nature, from that nature will reap destruction; the one who sows to please the Spirit, from the Spirit will reap eternal life" (Gal. 6:7-8).

When I think that my personality, looks, or abilities are my most important resources, take me back to the real source of strength: "'Not by might nor by power, but by my Spirit,' says the LORD Almighty" (Zech. 4:6).

When I gauge my progress by how close I am to the front of the line, teach me how You measure success: "If anyone wants to be first, he must be the very last, and the servant of all" (Mark 9:35).

When I assume that since I don't feel You, You're not here, gently remind me of Your steadfast vow: "Never will I leave you; never will I forsake you" (Heb. 13:5).

I will walk about in freedom, for I have sought out your precepts (Ps. 119:45).

Amen.

The Influencer

Don't let the world around you squeeze you into its own mould, but let
God re-make you so that your whole attitude of mind is changed. Thus
you will prove in practice that the will of God is good, acceptable to him
and perfect.

ROMANS 12:2, PHILLIPS

Gracious Lord,

Thank You for the grace You've shown to me. Your unfathomable mercies surround me constantly. I praise You, Lord!

You are worthy to receive my body as a living sacrifice, set apart for You alone (Rom. 12:1). But I need Your help to break the influence of my mutinous self and the manipulative world around me.

Please be the influencer of my being and doing today. Completely remold me today as You please. You created me with a fulfilling and significant life plan in mind (Eph. 2:10). Shape my thoughts and desires and deeds to accomplish Your will today.

Your purposes for me are only good (Jer. 29:11). Even Your discipline is only kind (Heb. 12:5-6). Help me see through the world's glittering deceptions—they promise bliss but deliver only trouble (Prov. 14:22).

Move me toward the goal of true maturity today—to be transformed into Your beautiful likeness (Rom. 12:2; 2 Cor. 3:18).

Amen.

Add It Up

*His divine power has given us everything we need for life and godliness
through our knowledge of him who called us by his own glory and
goodness.*

2 PETER 1:3

PRAYING FROM 2 PETER 1

Dear Lord Jesus,

Thank You that You've invited me to live an entirely new kind of life,
and You've also provided the power and the goodness to accomplish it
(v. 3). Today I praise You for this double provision: the royal title, and
the royal person to go with it. No matter what my past would say about
me, or what my own personality would try to dictate now, I can "par-
ticipate in the divine nature" (v. 4).

Help me to do my part to be a productive member of Your family
(v. 8). I want to bring honor, not shame, to Your reputation today.
Teach me from Your Word how to build, block by block, a life that's
worthy of my new identity. "Make every effort," Peter writes, to add:

—*goodness* (v. 5). Let Your goodness flow through me today like a
river of grace, bringing hope and healing to others (2 Cor. 9:8).

—*knowledge* (v. 5). Am I still in the dark about an issue? Shine
Your light of understanding, Holy Spirit. Open my eyes to the very
thing I might be trying hardest not to see and deal with.

—*self-control* (v. 6). Mold my will around the simple, necessary disciplines of right living. Even You can't work when I hang on to weakness, laziness, or fear (2 Tim. 1:7).

—*perseverance* (v. 6). I want to endure, by Your grace; to not become weary in doing what You ask, because in Your perfect timing, I'll reap a harvest of good if I don't give up (Gal. 6:9).

—*godliness* (v. 6). Not just for a good day, not just to be a better person, but to be like You—this is my request. To see reproduced in my life, Your life. For everyone I meet, let my presence be a touch of Yours today.

—*brotherly kindness* (v. 7). How great is the love You have lavished on me, that I can be called "child of God"—both a child and an heir (1 John 3:1; Rom. 8:17)! Show me how to build up my brothers and sisters today, to be a family member who makes a difference.

—*love* (v. 7). For every virtue and attitude I possess, help me to add love. Your love emanating from the core of my being can cover grievances and disappointments, heal hurts, bring encouragement, and be the final proof to all that I belong to You (1 John 4:7).

Thank You, Lord, that You've give me everything I need to "add it up" today.

In Your name I pray.

Amen.

The Good Lord

You are good, and what you do is good; teach me your decrees.

O Lord,

Truly, You are good all through. I've seen it in my life and in my family. I read about it in Your Word. Every page tells me these two incredible truths: You are strong, and You care (Ps. 62:11-12). I praise You today that You have both the intent to do good and the power to accomplish it exactly as You wish! I exalt You and honor You, Lord.

I praise You for Your loving acts on behalf of every person on earth. You are the One who satisfies the thirsty and fills the hungry with good things (Ps. 107:8).

You are forgiving and good, O Lord, abounding in love to all who call to you (Ps. 86:5).

I praise You that in my times of trouble You are a personal refuge for all those who trust in You (Nah. 1:7). You are good to those who run to You with their deepest longings and needs (Lam. 3:25).

I thank You that Your favor won't suddenly disappear. You are unalterably kind and trustworthy from generation to generation (Ps. 100:5).

I marvel that You, Most High, are even kind to those who are ungrateful and willfully evil (Luke 6:35). Today I remember You for who You are and worship You. May I see You in a fresh light all day long.

I will cause all my goodness to pass in front of you, and I will proclaim my name, the LORD, in your presence (Exod. 33:19).

Thank You, good Lord.

Amen.

Desire of My Heart

My soul yearns for you in the night; in the morning my spirit longs for you.

ISAIAH 26:9

Dear God,

You are the name of my deepest, most enduring longings. Forgive me that I sometimes meet those longings with quick-fix counterfeits: pleasure, power, style, money, or possessions. "Turn my eyes away from worthless things; preserve my life according to your word" (Ps. 119:37).

When I look for Your presence, I want to look beyond Your kind provisions of art, play, church, sex, family, nature, fitness, or even the joy of doing good. Why? Because "My heart says of you, 'Seek his face!' Your face, LORD, I will seek. Do not hide your face from me" (Ps. 27:8-9).

Without You, I'm always incomplete, unsatisfied, in transit. Today, I will stop looking in the wrong direction. "I will search for the one my heart loves" (Song of Songs 3:2).

Yes, You are my desire. It is not Your gifts I seek now, Lord. Or Your provisions, Your answers, or Your intervention. It's You. "O God, you are my God, earnestly I seek you; my soul thirsts for you, my body longs for you" (Ps. 63:1).

Dear God, show me Yourself today, in Jesus first of all (John 14:9). Then help me to see You in other ways: in Your Word, in others, in my thoughts, in my circumstances, in the world around me. It's so good to be near You (Ps. 73:28)!

You will seek me and find me when you seek me with all your heart. I will be found by you (Jer. 29:13-14).

Thank You, desire of my heart.

Amen.

The Soul's Paradox

To have found God and still to pursue Him is the soul's paradox of love, scorned indeed by the too-easily-satisfied religionist, but justified in happy experience by the children of the burning heart.

A. W. TOZER

The Gift of Gladness

A happy heart makes the face cheerful, but heartache crushes the spirit.

PROVERBS 15:13

Lord Jesus,

Today help me to be a gift of gladness for others.

You understand what it's like to be crushed in spirit. On earth You felt heartache and abandonment, homelessness and rejection, pain and anguish. And on top of it all, You cared for and carried our griefs when You died (Isa. 53:3-4). No wonder we can call You the "God of all comfort" (2 Cor. 1:3-4)!

Show me how to be Your hands and feet—giving an encouraging word or touch at just the right moment.

Give me the kind of wise insight that comes only from you (James 1:5). Help me to bless others with optimism and strong words of hope (Prov. 15:30). Don't let me miss the opportunities to share the wonderful comfort You've give me so many times (2 Cor. 1:3-4).

In Your name I pray.

Amen.

Working "As Though"

Work hard and cheerfully at whatever you do, as though you were
working for the Lord rather than for people.

Heavenly Father,

It's an illusion that good things happen without effort. But the book of
Proverbs says:

—"The sluggard craves and gets nothing, while the desires of the
diligent are fully satisfied" (13:4).

—"Hard work brings a profit, but mere talk leads only to poverty"
(14:23).

—"The one who chases fantasies will have his fill of poverty" (28:19).

Save me from the dead ends of laziness, fantasies, and "mere talk."
Grow in me a passion to be one who gets things done, who doesn't just
sit back and expect someone else to carry the load (2 Thess. 3:10).

Today I give You the labor of my hands and my mind as an act of
faith and worship. You know my needs exactly, Father, and this is the
day You've made for me. I'll rejoice and be glad in it (Ps. 118:24)!

Teach me the faith of Noah, who worked for years to build an ark for
his family when no water was in sight (Gen. 6:13-17; Heb. 11:7); the
humility of Ruth, who gleaned day after day so her mother-in-law could
be provided for (Ruth 2); and the passion of Jacob, who herded sheep for
fourteen years so he could earn the right to marry Rachel (Gen. 29:18-30).

Help me today to welcome tasks enthusiastically and without com-
plaining (Phil. 2:14). Why? Because I'm doing everything as though
You were my Lord and Master (Col. 3:23). And You are!

Amen.

Four "Ifs"

Remember Jesus Christ, raised from the dead, descended from David.
This is my gospel, for which I am suffering.

PRAYING FROM 2 TIMOTHY 2

Lord Jesus,

Direct my thoughts this morning as I meditate on Paul's "gospel":

If we died with him, we will also live with him (v. 11). Lord Jesus, I let go again of all those earth-bound desires and self-centered priorities. Thank You for Your life-giving gospel, even though it starts with the pain of death. "If anyone is in Christ, he is a new creation; the old has gone, the new has come!" (2 Cor. 5:17).

If we endure, we will also reign with him (v. 12). Lord Jesus, what is it You ask me to endure today? Thank You for Your power and Your promise that I will one day reign with you. "Blessed is the man who perseveres under trial, because when he has stood the test, he will receive the crown of life that God has promised to those who love him" (James 1:12).

If we disown him, he will also disown us (v. 12). Lord Jesus, so many around me disown You. Your message is antiquated, too hard, too exclusive, they say. Show me how I, too, disown You in thought or deed: by acting as if You are not Lord, by giving to another power in my life credit that belongs to You, by proposing that I don't need You. You gave Your life for me; help me release my life completely back to You. "We are not of those who shrink back and are destroyed, but of those who believe and are saved" (Heb. 10:39).

If we are faithless, he will remain faithful, for he cannot disown himself (v. 13). Lord Jesus, thank You that You are trustworthy even when I am not, that You are invested personally in my new life. "The Lord is faithful and he will do it" (from 2 Thess. 3:3).

Help me to remember and live these truths from moment to moment today.

Amen.

Wise Up

My son, if your heart is wise, then my heart will be glad;
my inmost being will rejoice when your lips speak what is right.

PROVERBS 23:15-16

PRAYING FROM PROVERBS

Dear Lord,

Thank You that Your care for Your children extends beyond big truths like salvation and eternal life to the everyday realities: getting your money's worth (Prov. 13:11), being a welcome neighbor (25:17), keeping your job (22:29), raising kids (22:6), and winning a good reputation (12:8).

You are the wisdom-source I need to build a life worth living (2:6). You've promised that if I seek wisdom with my whole heart, its practical, life-affirming, time-proven power will:

—lead me to success in business, at home, and in my private life (2:7)

—help me live in safety (2:8)

—surround me with protection from destructive relationships and dangerous situations (2:11)

—help me to live every day at ease, without fear (1:33)

—bring me a wealth more precious than gold and material wealth too (3:14,9-10)

But some things this world values as smart and obvious are actually a complete waste in Your sight (1 Cor. 3:19). For example, help me to put these all-American "virtues" under Your renewing influence today: being self-reliant (Prov. 3:5), speaking my mind (17:28), keeping score (19:11), and making sure I get the credit I deserve (27:2).

Rather, may Your Spirit lead me in life strategies that really work, like:

—"Let love and faithfulness never leave you" (3:3).

—"Shun evil" (3:7).

—"Honor the LORD with the firstfruits of your wealth" (3:9).

As I trust in You with all my heart, acknowledge You as God of my life, and don't lean on my own abilities or solutions, I know You'll lead me safely on (3:5-6). Thank You, Lord.

Please shape my thinking and my doing with wisdom today. Just any good idea or popular assumption won't do; I choose the wisdom of heaven (James 3:17). I want to make Your heart glad.

Amen.

Making an Impression

Now you have a king as your leader. As for me, I am old and gray....
Here I stand. Testify against me in the presence of the LORD and his
anointed. Whose ox have I taken?... Whom have I cheated? Whom have
I oppressed? From whose hand have I accepted a bribe to make me shut
my eyes? If I have done any of these, I will make it right.

1 SAMUEL 12:2-3

Heavenly Father,
What a day that was—Old Gray Beard himself stepping down, Israel's
first king stepping up. Everyone was so excited, not about Samuel's
speech or his service or even his record of integrity, but about the status
the nation would now have as a kingdom with its very own royal family. And what a stunning specimen was King Saul: "an impressive young
man without equal among the Israelites—a head taller than any of the
others" (1 Sam. 9:2).

But how soon their "impressive" king let them down, led the
nation into turmoil, left the words of the old prophet to echo in their
memories...

Lord, I do want to be an impressive person—to You, to those I
love, to those who depend on me. But when I make my stand, let it be
like Samuel's—on a lifetime of integrity. Not like Saul's—on appearances only.

Almost everyone can be impressive before the time of testing
(1 Pet. 2:19-21). But Your Word says, "The noble man makes noble
plans, and by noble deeds he stands" (Isa. 32:8). That's the kind of life
I want to build. Through Your grace and power, and by my daily

commitment, I want to live a life worthy of my calling in Jesus Christ (Eph. 4:1).

Thank You for men like Samuel, who refused to take advantage of his position to defraud his people. Teach me from the gallery of other heroes (truly impressive believers) who have gone before me:

—Job, who maintained his integrity even in the face of bankruptcy, grief, shame, illness, and death (Job 2:3)

—Esther, who risked execution rather than live luxuriously in a lie (Esther 4:14-16)

—Daniel, whose enemies found nothing to say against him because "he was trustworthy and neither corrupt nor negligent" (Dan. 6:4)

—Timothy, who guarded what had been entrusted to him, and held on to "faith and a good conscience" (1 Tim. 1:19; 6:20)

Today, help me to take small steps in the right direction. Help me to focus my thoughts and energies on what will make an impression for eternity. Please ferret out those slippery thieves of integrity: duplicity (Prov. 11:3), lying (Jer. 5:1), tolerating sin (1 Tim. 5:24-25), and refusing to face hard truths (Prov. 27:6).

Thank You that through Christ I have "put on the new self, which is being renewed in knowledge in the image of its Creator" (Col. 3:10). Do Your renewing work every day of my life, Father.

I ask these things in Your Son's name.

Amen.

The Renewing Presence

We do not lose heart. Though outwardly we are wasting away, yet inwardly we are being renewed day by day.

2 CORINTHIANS 4:16

Holy Spirit,

You are always at work. You are always here. You are always nudging, prompting, guiding, talking... I see You at work, invisible Spirit, and I love You. I meditate on Your renewing presence today.

You are God's abiding expression of love to me. Holy Spirit, how I thank and worship You (Rom. 5:5).

You are Jesus' promised gift of comfort to me. Spirit of Comfort, thank You that You'll never leave (John 14:16).

You are the Truth that lives in me. Spirit of Truth, grant me Your insights in my choices and help me live by the truth today (John 14:7,17).

You are my advocate and interpreter in heaven today. You help me speak to God my Father. In my earthbound weakness, You pray for me in a God-made language I don't know and always ask for what God most wants to give (Rom. 8:27). Holy Spirit, pray for me today—pray through me. Take my groans and lapses and self-absorbed thoughts and shape them into God-infused priorities.

You are the Spirit of power, promised by Jesus to help me live out the gospel every day. I want to live and speak Christ's life boldly today (Acts 4:31). Holy Spirit, enter my body, Your temple right now. Yes, reign supreme, Holy Spirit. Take ownership of every impulse. I don't belong to me anymore (1 Cor. 6:19)!

Amen.

The Filling

ay the Holy Spirit fill you with

joy and peace today

as you put your trust in God.

And may His hope flood your being

and overflow to others, too.

from Romans 15:13

Escape Route

No temptation has seized you except what is common to man. And God is faithful; he will not let you be tempted beyond what you can bear. But when you are tempted, he will also provide a way out so that you can stand up under it.

Heavenly Father,

Today I'm up against forces far stronger than I am, and I desperately need Your help. Powerful and destructive enticements pull me away from You. I'm not proud of the truth, but I know it comes as no shock to You—You know me completely.

Rescue me, my God! I can almost hear Satan roaring like a lion in my ear (1 John 2:16; 1 Pet. 5:8). Don't let evil injure me (Ps. 31:4).

Show me an escape route today, as you've promised. Lead me firmly away from temptation (Matt. 6:13). By your power, block the wrong people from influencing my desires and actions (Ps. 140:1). Help me see through these "opportunities" for what they really are— death traps (James 1:15).

Turn my eyes away from worthless things; renew my life according to your Word (Ps. 119:37). Bring Your Word, hidden in my memory, into my thoughts; use it to keep me from sin (Ps. 119:11).

My God, all attractions but You fade away (Ps. 102:12). Show me today that the one who obeys You lives best, both now and in eternity (1 John 2:17; Ps. 16:11).

In the saving name of Jesus I pray. Amen.

Jacob's Limp

Jacob was left alone, and a man wrestled with him till daybreak....
Then the man said, "Let me go, for it is daybreak." But Jacob replied, "I
will not let you go unless you bless me." The man asked him, "What is
your name?" "Jacob," he answered. Then the man said, "Your name will
no longer be Jacob ['striver'], but Israel ['he struggles with God'], because
you have struggled with God and with men and have overcome."...
Then he blessed him there. So Jacob called the place Peniel, saying, "It is
because I saw God face to face, and yet my life was spared." The sun rose
above him as he passed Peniel, and he was limping.

GENESIS 32:24-31

Heavenly Father,
You've certainly chosen some peculiar, cantankerous, generally
unpromising, and frequently impossible people to be Your children.
Like Jacob. Like me. Your pursuing love is a wonder to me today.

Help me learn from Jacob, who struggled to get Your best. Was it
arrogance and greed that made him grunt and strain in the dirt with
that Angel all night? Or did he really believe—was there a settled confidence in his spirit—that his God was kind and generous and powerful
enough that that kind of intimate, strenuous confrontation with Him
could only bring good? You did lavish good on Jacob (Gen. 46:2-7).

I'm surrounded by competitors: They want perfect bodies, trophy
houses and spouses, gold medals. "No pain, no gain," they say.

But Father, I humbly pray for Jacob's limp. With Paul, I pray, "To
this end I labor, struggling with all his energy, which so powerfully
works in me" (Col. 1:29). Yes, may others look at me and see I've paid
the price to get God's best. Amen.

God's Prisoner

As the Lord's prisoner, then, I beg you to live lives worthy of your high calling. Accept life with humility and patience, generously making allowances for each other because you love each other.

EPHESIANS 4:1-2, PHILLIPS

Lord God,

My highest ambition today is to be Your prisoner. (It's the only genuine freedom.) Just yesterday I asked, "If God is in this, why is it so hard?" But I see that I was looking at things all wrong. You work through hard things, too.

Today I acknowledge Your irresistible power and Your unfailing goodness (Ps. 62:11-12). You are Lord of every difficult thing (every iron bar, gray wall, rusty lock, and rat in my life).

When being a Christian sets me up for ridicule, You are graciously giving to me a shared identity with Jesus, my suffering Savior (Phil. 3:10).

When hardships or difficult relationships seem to batter me, You are lovingly disciplining me so that You can produce a harvest of good and well-being through me and for me (Heb. 12:11).

When evil persons seem to have the upper hand, You are not surprised or mocked or threatened. It's good to wait patiently for You, Lord, experiencing the peace that comes from knowing that You are in control and that You delight in me (Ps. 37:1-7,23)!

When the answers I've pleaded for don't come, You are answering out of my sight. (I must live by faith.) You've promised me good all the days of my life. And You never lie (John 14:13-14; Eph. 3:20; Rom. 8:28; Heb. 6:18).

When my personal resources are stretched beyond my limits, I declare that it is You lovingly at work. In my limitations and weaknesses, You are finding opportunities to be strong. In my struggles, Your hands are busy shaping and re-creating me into the likeness of Jesus (2 Cor. 12:9; Eph. 4:14-15).

When Satan seems to have lined up his hostile legions against me, I can find complete security knowing that You've already defeated him at the Cross—and it's just a matter of time before he's put away for good (Col. 2:15; 1 John 3:8).

Even if nothing in my life seems to add up and I die in the "prison" of suffering or unrealized goals, You have all eternity to make things right. You've promised to reward me with Your grace, justice, and generosity and to do so face to face (Luke 6:20-23; 1 John 3:1-2)!

That is why I affirm today that I am not a victim of any person, power, or circumstance. You are Lord, and that can change every prison into a cathedral of praise.

Amen.

A Prayer for God's Family

I kneel before the Father, from whom his whole family in heaven and on earth derives its name.

EPHESIANS 3:14-15

PRAYING FROM EPHESIANS 3

Heavenly Father,
I join Paul today in his prayer for believers. I pray for myself as Your child, for Christians I love, and for Your church around the world.

I kneel before the Father, from whom his whole family in heaven and on earth derives its name (Eph. 3:14-15). Yes, Lord, Your name is on us; we are Yours. We're "set apart," "chosen," "children of God," extravagantly blessed with the heritage of those who love Your name—"Father God." What a privilege to be so honored! I kneel in adoration before You (Isa. 43:1; 1 Pet. 2:9; 1 John 3:1; Ps. 61:5).

I pray that out of his glorious riches he may strengthen you with power through his Spirit in your inner being, so that Christ may dwell in your hearts through faith (Eph. 3:16-17). As Your offspring, may we show a family likeness by allowing the Spirit complete control over our choices and desires. May character traits like love, joy, peace, patience, kindness, goodness, faithfulness, gentleness, and self-control be abundantly evident in our lives today. We can't complete through our own energies what was begun by faith in Your power (Gal. 5:16-23; 3:3; Rom. 1:16-17).

And I pray that you, being rooted and established in love, may have power, together with all the saints (Eph. 3:17-18). Yes, let love be the family trademark. Love that changes us; that motivates us to live in more redemptive ways than even "human goodness" would suggest. May I and all Christians today put down our roots in Your Word and in regular fellowship with other believers. Only a selfless caring about Your people and Your world can make any difference. Only loves lasts (Mark 12:30-33; John 15:9-10).

To grasp how wide and long and high and deep is the love of Christ, and to know this love that surpasses knowledge (Eph. 3:18-19). Before we pick up one worry or fear today, help us to experience a new understanding of the immensity of Your love, O God. Like Paul, may we be fully persuaded that nothing on earth is greater, stronger, or more significant to us personally than the love of Christ (Rom. 8:38-39).

That you may be filled to the measure of all the fullness of God (Eph. 3:19). Yes, fill us with all of You! With Augustine I pray, "O Lord, the house of my soul is narrow; enlarge it, that You may enter in."[1] We have no idea what that could mean for us even today, but "fullness of God" is our everyday heritage as Your children. And surely it's the beginning of what You want for us today—to do immeasurably more than all we ask or imagine, because Your power is at work in us (from v. 20).

May every generation of Your children on this planet bring You glory, Father! May Jesus' name be praised because of what Christians say and do today (v. 21)—at home, in church, and around the world.

Amen.

The Treasures of Fearing God

He will be the sure foundation for your times, a rich store of salvation
and wisdom and knowledge; the fear of the LORD is the key to this
treasure.

ISAIAH 33:6

Lord of heaven,
I want the world from You, but I treat You all wrong. I'm so sorry.

I treat you like an insurance policy to cover "eventualities" if something happens. I treat you like a blankie, to drag around and fondle when I'm feeling insecure.

I treat you like my personal bodyguard to keep the bad guys at bay, or even the score when I'm knocked down.

I treat you like a vending machine, to give me what I want when I want it—no fuss, no muss.

I treat you like an imaginary friend, conjuring You up in my imagination when I need You and forgetting about You the rest of the time.

I treat You like a flashlight. I click open Your Word if I need help or direction, then I click off and close my eyes and ears, and put You away in the drawer.

I treat You like a baby playing peekaboo. If I can't see You, I pretend You can't see me. That way it doesn't feel so bad when I stride about my life as if I—not You—were the center of it.

Lord of Heaven, why do I treat You this way? Could it be that I don't remember (in my deepest awareness and conviction) who You are? If I did, I would treat You completely different.

I would tremble in awe at Your power.

I would kneel reverently in Your presence all day long.

I would lie on my face when I recount my offenses.

I would listen in reverent anticipation of a word from You.

I would truly love Your name.

Lord of all, I think I do love You. Pardon my unpardonable, infantile faith. Open to me the treasures of fearing You today:

—If I will hold you in awe, the goodness You've stored up for me will be immeasurable, and I won't have to grab it for myself (Ps. 31:19).

—If I will bend my will, my loyalties, my priorities to You and Your revealed truths, my life will bubble up like a fountain, running over, splashing down with plenty (Prov. 14:27).

—If I will acknowledge and respond to You as the still point of my turning world, You will guide and instruct me in the perfect way You chose for me long ago (Ps. 25:8; Eph. 2:10).

—If I will worship You as God above all gods, and God above me, You will take me into Your confidence, talking to me personally about what really matters in life (Ps. 25:14).

If you fear me and honor My name and place all your hopes in who I really am, I will delight in you. I will give You everything you need. I will redeem you and call you "My treasured possession" (from Ps. 147:11; Psalm 128; Mal. 3:16-17).

Thank You, loving, patient and merciful Lord of heaven. You alone are worthy of worship. You make the mountains melt like wax and the oceans roar, "The LORD reigns!" (Ps. 97:5; 1 Chron. 16:31).

And right now You make my spirit tremble like a reed in the wind with fear and gladness.

Amen.

Something New

As surely as the sun rises, he will appear; he will come to us like the
winter rains, like the spring rains that water the earth.

Lord God,

Work, drive, meals, kids, church, cleanup, back to work—that's my life!
What used to sparkle with meaning has faded into routine. I feel like
the writer of Ecclesiastes: "All things are wearisome, more than one can
say.... What has been will be again, what has been done will be done
again; there is nothing new under the sun" (Eccles. 1:8-9).

Even the relationships that matter most to me have turned various
shades of gray: repetitious conversations, predictable reactions, length-
ening pauses... How I long for something new today!

Are You doing anything new here? I know You can. Underneath
whatever I can see, You are at work transforming me into Your likeness
"with ever-increasing glory" (2 Cor. 3:18). You are the God who can
make all things new (Rev. 21:5). Please do!

If I'm too busy looking back, dreaming of how things used to be or
ought to be, turn my head around. You have a miracle waiting *today*. If
my stubbornness or laziness is in the way of a new thing you are trying
to accomplish, show me, Lord.

Today I choose to watch and wait for new green growth, for
swelling buds of hope. I don't want to miss the wonderful signs of Your
presence.

Amen.

Unforgettable!

Can a mother forget the baby at her breast and have no compassion on the child she has borne? Though she may forget, I will not forget you! See, I have engraved you on the palms of my hands.

ISAIAH 49:15-16

Mighty God,

Thank You for Your promises that my children are unforgettable to You.

—*You will fight for my children.* Even if fierce adversaries of any kind capture them, You will win them back. You've declared, "I will contend with those who contend with you, and your children I will save!" (Isa. 49:24-25). I claim Your promise today against the wrong crowd, negative media and cultural influences, unhealthy value systems, and any kind of destructive power. Thank You, Lord.

—*You won't let my children become lost.* You promise to retrieve my sons and daughters from "the ends of the earth," if necessary, because they are called by Your name and created for Your glory (Isa. 43:5-7). I claim this promise today for their whole life. There are so many ways to get "lost": in success, in things, in relationships, in trends, in self… Thank You, loving God, that You'll pursue them and bring them home.

—*You will pour out Your Holy Spirit on my children.* Your new life will spring up in them "like grass in a meadow, like poplar trees by flowing streams," and they will identify themselves as Yours (from Isa. 44:3-5).

I trust these promises today, Lord, and I trust You! I worship You for Your kindness.

Amen.

Climbing Tools

Who may ascend the hill of the LORD? Who may stand in his holy place?

PRAYING FROM PSALM 24

Heavenly Father,

How can I ascend into Your holy presence today? Your Word lays out my "climbing tools":

Clean hands. What have I done that's offended You or others? What have I left undone that I should have done? Show me, God. Forgive me of my sins. Wash away all the stains on my record (1 John 1:9).

A pure heart. What about my thoughts and intentions? So often I look good on the outside, but my heart reveals me as a fake. Forgive me, Lord. Create in me a pure heart (Ps. 51:10).

Does not worship idols. What other influence or power determines how I spend my time and my money? What other person or possession comes first in my affections? Show me, Lord. Only You are worthy of that kind of control in my life (1 Pet. 3:15).

Does not swear falsely. What other person or source do I look to for help to live my life and keep my promises? Reveal my dependencies, Father. You are the only entirely trustworthy refuge and deliverer (Ps. 118:8-9).

Thank You that whether I deserve to come into Your presence or not, I'm always welcome because I'm Your child. Jesus' perfect goodness covers me! He is my high priest and advocate with You, Righteous King (1 Cor. 1:30; 1 Tim. 2:5).

Amen.

Panorama of Hope

You do not even know what will happen tomorrow. What is your life?
You are a mist that appears for a little while and then vanishes.

JAMES 4:14

Heavenly Father,

The view from here is just another bend in the road. Just another distance disappearing in the haze. I can't see past today. But You are the Lord of time: A day is like a thousand years to You, and You never change (2 Pet. 3:8; Heb. 13:8). I can safely commit my future into Your powerful and loving care.

Father, I give You my tomorrows, along with all of today's questions, doubts, joys, and tears. I give You all my dreams and disappointments. But it's an entirely hopeful surrender because I can be confident You'll finish the good work You've started in my life (Phil. 1:6).

I confess I sometimes panic, cry out, try to make things happen by myself. But remind me that You, Almighty God, are always at work in me to help me want and to help me accomplish a life that honors You (Phil. 2:13). Your plan is incredible: to realize in me and for me and through me for others "a hope and a future" (Jer. 29:11)!

Thank You that when You say "future," You don't mean just putting in time, but that the days and years ahead for me will have great purpose. And when You say "hope," You don't just refer to an emotion, but to something sure—and to Someone worth living for.

Do not be anxious about tomorrow. Commit your way to Me. Trust in Me and I will act (from Matt. 6:34; Ps. 37:5).

Thank You, God of tomorrow. I trust You.

Amen.

Treasure Hunt

So we fix our eyes not on what is seen, but on what is unseen.
For what is seen is temporary, but what is unseen is eternal

2 CORINTHIANS 4:18

Lord,

My value sensors are unreliable, my eyes half-blind. My carnal impulses latch on to every bauble. But my soul was made to soar.

Today, by Your new life at work in my being, help me to recognize the difference between an earthly and a heavenly treasure: Can it break, rust, or outwear its warranty? Is it collectible for only a while (Matt. 6:19-21)? Or is it something invisible that I can build my life on, now and for eternity—like salvation, God's favor, peace, and joy (2 Cor. 4:18)?

Oh, I'm bombarded by slick appeals to my comfort, greed, and vanity. My wants are insatiable. Is my highest purpose here to "eat, drink, and be merry"? No! You died for a better reason, Holy Lord.

Fix my attention today! Yet, fix it on the real values in this "treasure hunt" of life. I don't want to serve money, fame, or pleasure. They suck the life out of me and split my loyalties. Help me identify these idols and throw them out. I want to serve You alone (Matt. 6:24).

Spend your energy seeking the eternal life that I…can give you (John 6:27, NLT).

Lord, lead me to the treasure that lasts.

Amen.

Convinced!

In all these things we are more than conquerors through him who loved us.

ROMANS 8:37

PRAYING FROM ROMANS 8

Heavenly Lord,

You're ready to make circumstances work out for good if I follow You (v. 28). And because You're for me in this way, it doesn't matter who's against me (v. 31). Your Cross stands against the sky of my life as a personal guarantee: Nothing can separate me from Your love!

I am convinced that neither death nor life,

(not car wrecks, cancer, muggings, drug habits, aneurysms, or old age)

neither angels nor demons,

(not doomsday cults, oppressive spirits, shock jocks, or porn shops)

neither the present nor the future,

(not late-breaking crises or millennial threats)

nor any powers,

(not oppressive governments, crazed dictators, abusive bosses, or inconsiderate spouses)

neither height nor depth,

(not wealth, fame, and accomplishment—or poverty, shame, and failure)

nor anything else in all creation,

(not FDA warnings, global warming, faulty plumbing, how badly I'm failing, or whatever else it is I worry about at 4 A.M.)

will be able to separate me from the love of God

that is in Christ Jesus my Lord!

Amen!

Notes

AN INVITATION

1   David M. Dawson, *More Power in Prayer* (Grand Rapids, Mich.:
    Zondervan, 1942), 104.

2   François Fénelon, quoted in *A Guide to Prayer,* ed. Reuben P.
    Job and Morman Shawchuck (Nashville: Upper Room Books,
    1983), 56.

THE CONVERSATION OF YOUR LIFE

1   A. W. Tozer, *The Pursuit of God* (Harrisburg, Penn.: Christian
    Publications, 1948), 11.

2   *The Book of Common Prayer* (Kingsport, Tenn.: Kingsport Press,
    1977), 336.

3   C. S. Lewis, *The Joyful Christian* (New York: Macmillan, 1977),
    86, quoted in Bob Benson Sr. and Michael W. Benson, *Disciplines
    for the Inner Life* (Nashville: Generoux/Nelson, 1989), 272.

4   Mother Teresa, *My Life for the Poor,* ed. José Luis Gonzalez-
    Balado and Janet N. Playfoot (San Francisco: Harper & Row,
    1985), 49.

5   Wayne Spear, *The Theology of Prayer* (Grand Rapids, Mich.:
    Baker, 1979), 59-60.

6   Henri J. M. Nouwen, *With Open Hands* (New York: Ballantine Books/Epiphany, 1985), 3-8.

7   Richard J. Foster, *Prayers from the Heart* (San Francisco: Harper San Francisco, 1994), xiv.

DAILY PRAYERS

1   Carol Plueddeman and Vinita Hampton Wright, eds., *Prayers Around the Family Table* (Wheaton, Ill.: Harold Shaw, 1992), 21.

QUOTATIONS *(referenced by page number)*

21   A. W. Tozer, "Missing Jewel," *Essays on Prayer* (Downers Grove, Ill.: InterVarsity, 1968), 9-10.

28   C. S. Lewis, *Surprised by Joy* (New York: Harcourt Brace Jovanovich, 1955), 228-9.

37   Julian of Norwich, quoted in Vinita Hampton Wright, *Prayers Across the Centuries* (Wheaton, Ill.: Harold Shaw, 1993), 80.

41   Roy Hicks Jr., *A Small Book About God* (Sisters, Oreg.: Multnomah, 1997), 125-6.

51   David McKenna, no source available.

61   Paul Tournier, "Reflections," quoted in Bob Benson Sr. and Michael W. Benson, *Disciplines of the Inner Life* (Nashville: Nelson/Generoux, 1989), 224.

67   Amy Carmichael, quoted in Terry W. Glaspey, *Pathway to the Heart of God* (Eugene, Oreg.: Harvest House, 1998), 139.

75   Lloyd John Ogilvie, *Praying with Power* (Ventura, Calif.: Regal, 1983), 12.

81   Richard Foster, *Celebration of Discipline* (New York: Harper & Row, 1978), 30.

95   A. W. Tozer, *The Pursuit of God* (Harrisburg, Penn.: Christian Publications, 1948), 9-10.

116 Armin Gesswein, no source available.

123 Leanne Payne, *Listening Prayer* (Grand Rapids, Mich.: Baker, 1994), 27.

143 Payne, *Listening Prayer*, 122.

153 Anselm, quoted in Ken Gire, *Between Heaven and Earth* (San Francisco: HarperSanFrancisco, 1997), 105.

159 Simon Tugwell, *Prayer: Living with God* (Springfield, Ill.: Templegate Publishers, 1975), 14.

169 C. Peter Wagner, *Prayer Shield* (Ventura, Calif.: Regal, 1992), 26, 50.

173 Tozer, "Missing Jewel," 4-6.

180 Tozer, *The Pursuit of God*, 15.

Title Index

Topical Index

To contact the author:
David Kopp
P. O. Box 723
Sisters, OR 97759
(541) 549-4246
davidkopp@aol.com